Why This Book Is Important

ROI Fundamentals, the first book in the Measurement and Evaluation Series, introduces the ROI Methodology, a methodical approach to evaluation that can be replicated throughout an organization, enabling comparisons of results between one program and another. The process described in this book is the most documented method in the world, and its application has been phenomenal, with over five thousand individuals participating in five-day certification programs designed for implementation. Although other books may delve into accountability in certain types of programs or data, this book introduces a method that works across all types of programs, ranging from leadership development to basic skills training for new employees. With this approach, every program is evaluated at some level. With executives asking for more accountability from program leaders and teams, the information in this book—and series—is critical.

Evaluating Program Value

This book introduces a results-based approach to program implementation, focusing on a variety of measures, categorized into seven data types:

1. Inputs and indicators
2. Reaction and planned action
3. Learning and confidence
4. Application and implementation

5. Impact and consequences

6. Return on investment

7. Intangible benefits

ROI Fundamentals describes a process that will help those challenged with implementing and evaluating programs to identify, collect, analyze, and report all seven types of data in a consistent manner that ensures credible results.

How This Book Is Organized

This book introduces and follows the value chain of program evaluation throughout the program cycle. Chapter One, "A Brief Description of the ROI Methodology," introduces the ROI Methodology discussed throughout the remainder of this series. Chapter Two, "Why ROI? Key Issues and Trends," discusses why program evaluation and measurement (up to and including ROI) and the move toward results-based measurement are currently so critical. It also discusses the barriers to the ROI Methodology and the benefits of the process. Chapter Three, "Who Should Use the ROI Methodology?" helps determine if an organization is a candidate for implementing the ROI Methodology.

Chapter Four, "How to Build a Credible Process," describes the ROI Methodology framework and the ROI process model, along with the operating standards and the implementation of the methodology. Chapter Five, "Inhibitors of Implementation," explains the many barriers to the implementation of the ROI Methodology. It lists these barriers and discusses ways to avoid or neutralize them. Many myths about the methodology, and also its realities, are included.

Finally, Chapter Six, "Planning for Evaluation," begins by discussing how to establish the purpose and feasibility of a program. Then it details the steps for developing program objectives and planning documents. The chapter ends by discussing how to conduct a planning meeting and how to identify data sources.

The Measurement and Evaluation Series

Editors

Patricia Pulliam Phillips, Ph.D.

Jack J. Phillips, Ph.D.

Introduction to the Measurement and Evaluation Series

The ROI Six Pack provides detailed information on developing ROI evaluations, implementing the ROI Methodology, and showing the value of a variety of functions and processes. With detailed examples, tools, templates, shortcuts, and checklists, this series will be a valuable reference for individuals interested in using the ROI Methodology to show the impact of their projects, programs, and processes.

The Need

Although financial ROI has been measured for over one hundred years to quantify the value of plants, equipment, and companies, the concept has only recently been applied to evaluate the impact of learning and development, human resources, technology, quality, marketing, and other support functions. In the learning and development field alone, the use of ROI has become routine in many organizations. In the past decade, hundreds of organizations have embraced the ROI process to show the impact of many different projects and programs.

Along the way, professionals and practitioners need help. They need tools, templates, and tips, along with explanations, examples, and details, to make this process work. Without this help, using the ROI Methodology to show the value of projects and programs is difficult. In short, practitioners need shortcuts and proven techniques to minimize the resources required to use this process. Practitioners' needs have created the need for this series. This series will provide the detail necessary to make the ROI Methodology successful within an organization. For easy reference and use, the books are logically arranged to align with the steps of the ROI Methodology.

Audience

The principal audience for these books is individuals who plan to use the ROI Methodology to show the value of their projects and programs. Such individuals are specialists or managers charged with proving the value of their particular project or program. They need detailed information, know-how, and confidence.

A second audience is those who have used the ROI Methodology for some time but want a quick reference with tips and techniques to make ROI implementation more successful within their organization. This series, which explains the evaluation process in detail, will be a valuable reference set for these individuals, regardless of other ROI publications owned.

A third audience is consultants and researchers who want to know how to address specific evaluation issues. Three important challenges face individuals as they measure ROI and conduct ROI evaluations: (1) collecting post-program data, (2) isolating the effects of the program, and (3) converting data to monetary values. A book is devoted to each of these critical issues, allowing researchers and consultants to easily find details on each issue.

A fourth audience is those who are curious about the ROI Methodology and its use. The first book in this series focuses specifically on ROI, its use, and how to determine whether it is appropriate for an organization. When interest is piqued, the remaining books provide more detail.

Flow of the Books

The six books are presented in a logical sequence, mirroring the ROI process model. Book one, *ROI Fundamentals: Why and When to Measure ROI*, presents the basic ROI Methodology and makes the business case for measuring ROI as it explores the benefits and barriers to implementation. It also examines the type of organization best suited for the ROI Methodology and the best time to implement it. Planning for an ROI evaluation is also explored in this book.

Book two, *Data Collection: Planning For and Collecting All Types of Data*, details data collection by examining the different techniques, methods, and issues involved in this process, with an emphasis on collecting post-program data. It examines the different data collection methods: questionnaires, interviews, focus groups, observation, action plans, performance contracts, and monitoring records.

Book three, *Isolation of Results: Defining the Impact of the Program*, focuses on the most valuable part of the ROI Methodology and the essential step for ensuring credibility. Recognizing that factors other than the program being measured can influence results, this book shows a variety of ways in which the effects of a program can be isolated from other influences. Techniques include comparison analysis using a control group, trend line analysis and forecasting methods, and expert input from a variety of sources.

Book four, *Data Conversion: Calculating the Monetary Benefits*, covers perhaps the second toughest challenge of ROI evaluation: placing monetary value on program benefits. To calculate the ROI, data must be converted to money, and *Data Conversion* shows how this conversion has been accomplished in a variety of organizations. The good news is that standard values are available for many items. When they are not, the book shows different techniques for converting them, ranging from calculating the value from records to seeking experts and searching databases. When data cannot be converted to money credibly and with minimum resources, they are considered intangible. This book explores the range of intangible benefits and the necessary techniques for collecting, analyzing, and recording them.

Book five, *Costs and ROI: Evaluating at the Ultimate Level*, focuses on costs and ROI. This book shows that all costs must be captured in order to create a fully loaded cost profile. All the costs must be included in order to be conservative and to give the analysis additional credibility. Next, the actual ROI calculation is presented, showing the various assumptions and issues that must be addressed when calculating the ROI. Three different calculations are presented: the benefit-cost ratio, the ROI percentage, and the payback period. The book concludes with several cautions and concerns about the use of ROI and its meaning.

Book six, *Communication and Implementation: Sustaining the Practice*, explores two important issues. The first issue is reporting the results of an evaluation. This is the final part of the ROI Methodology and is necessary to ensure that audiences have the information they need so that improvement processes can be implemented. A range of techniques is available, including face-to-face meetings, brief reports, one-page summaries, routine communications, mass-audience techniques, and electronic media. All are available for reporting evaluation results. The final part of the book focuses on how to sustain the ROI evaluation process: how to use it, keep it going, and make it work in the long term to add value to the organization and, often, to show the value of all the programs and projects within a function or department.

Terminology: Programs, Projects, Solutions

In this series the terms *program* and *project* are used to describe many processes that can be evaluated using the ROI Methodology. This is an important issue because readers may vary widely in their perspectives. Individuals involved in technology applications may

Table I.1. Terms and Applications

Term	Example
Program	Leadership development skills enhancement for senior executives
Project	A reengineering scheme for a plastics division
System	A fully interconnected network for all branches of a bank
Initiative	A faith-based effort to reduce recidivism
Policy	A new preschool plan for disadvantaged citizens
Procedure	A new scheduling arrangement for truck drivers
Event	A golf outing for customers
Meeting	A U.S. Coast Guard conference on innovations
Process	Quality sampling
People	Staff additions in the customer care center
Tool	A new means of selecting hotel staff

use the terms *system* and *technology* rather than *program* or *project*. In public policy, in contrast, the word *program* is prominent. For a professional meetings and events planner, the word *program* may not be pertinent, but in human resources, *program* is often used. Finding one term for all these situations would be difficult. Consequently, the terms *program* and *project* are used interchangeably. Table I.1 lists these and other terms that may be used in other contexts.

Features

Each book in the series takes a straightforward approach to make it understandable, practical, and useful. Checklists are provided, charts are included, templates are presented, and examples are explored. All are intended to show how the ROI Methodology works. The focus of these books is implementing the process and making it successful within an organization. The methodology is based on the work of hundreds of individuals who have made the ROI Methodology a successful evaluation process within their organizations.

About Pfeiffer

Pfeiffer serves the professional development and hands-on resource needs of training and human resource practitioners and gives them products to do their jobs better. We deliver proven ideas and solutions from experts in HR development and HR management, and we offer effective and customizable tools to improve workplace performance. From novice to seasoned professional, Pfeiffer is the source you can trust to make yourself and your organization more successful.

Essential Knowledge Pfeiffer produces insightful, practical, and comprehensive materials on topics that matter the most to training and HR professionals. Our Essential Knowledge resources translate the expertise of seasoned professionals into practical, how-to guidance on critical workplace issues and problems. These resources are supported by case studies, worksheets, and job aids and are frequently supplemented with CD-ROMs, Web sites, and other means of making the content easier to read, understand, and use.

Essential Tools Pfeiffer's Essential Tools resources save time and expense by offering proven, ready-to-use materials—including exercises, activities, games, instruments, and assessments—for use during a training or team-learning event. These resources are frequently offered in looseleaf or CD-ROM format to facilitate copying and customization of the material.

Pfeiffer also recognizes the remarkable power of new technologies in expanding the reach and effectiveness of training. While e-hype has often created whizbang solutions in search of a problem, we are dedicated to bringing convenience and enhancements to proven training solutions. All our e-tools comply with rigorous functionality standards. The most appropriate technology wrapped around essential content yields the perfect solution for today's on-the-go trainers and human resource professionals.

 Essential resources for training and HR professionals

www.pfeiffer.com

ROI Fundamentals

Why and When to Measure ROI

Patricia Pulliam Phillips, Ph.D.
Jack J. Phillips, Ph.D.

Pfeiffer

A Wiley Imprint

www.pfeiffer.com

Published by Pfeiffer
An Imprint of Wiley
989 Market Street, San Francisco, CA 94103-1741
www.pfeiffer.com

For additional copies/bulk purchases of this book in the U.S. please contact 800-274-4434.

Pfeiffer books and products are available through most bookstores. To contact Pfeiffer directly call our Customer Care Department within the U.S. at 800-274-4434, outside the U.S. at 317-572-3985, fax 317-572-4002, or visit www.pfeiffer.com.

Pfeiffer also publishes its books in a variety of electronic formats. Some content that appears in print may not be available in electronic books.

Library of Congress Cataloging-in-Publication Data

Phillips, Patricia Pulliam.
    ROI fundamentals: why and when to measure ROI/ Patricia Pulliam Phillips, Jack J. Phillips.
        p. cm.—(Measurement and evaluation series)
    Includes bibliographical references and index.
    ISBN: 978-0-7879-8716-9 (pbk.)
        1. Employees—Training of—Cost effectiveness. 2. Rate of return.
3. Project management—Evaluation.
I. Phillips, Jack J., date. II. Title. III. Title: Return on investments fundamentals.
HF5549.5.T7P437 2008
658.15′52—dc22

                                                                2007028787

Production Editor: Michael Kay   Editorial Assistant: Julie Rodriguez
Editor: Matthew Davis   Manufacturing Supervisor: Becky Morgan
Printed in the United States of America

PB Printing 10 9 8 7 6 5 4 3 2 1

Contents

Chapter 5: Inhibitors of Implementation   83

Chapter 6: Planning for Evaluation   99

Acknowledgments from the Editors

From Patti

No project, regardless of its size or scope, is completed without the help and support of others. My sincere thanks go to the staff at Pfeiffer. Their support for this project has been relentless. Matt Davis has been the greatest! It is our pleasure and privilege to work with such a professional and creative group of people.

Thanks also go to my husband, Jack. His unwavering support of my work is always evident. His idea for the series was to provide readers with a practical understanding of the various components of a comprehensive measurement and evaluation process. This first book sets the stage for that understanding. Thank you, Jack, for another fun opportunity!

From Jack

Many thanks go to the staff who helped make this series a reality. Lori Ditoro did an excellent job of meeting a very tight deadline and delivering a quality manuscript.

Much admiration and thanks go to Patti. She is an astute observer of the ROI Methodology, having observed and learned from hundreds of presentations, consulting assignments, and engagements. In addition, she is an excellent researcher and student of the process, studying how it is developed and how it works. She has become an ROI expert in her own right. Thanks, Patti, for your many contributions. You are a great partner, friend, and spouse.

Preface: The Realities of ROI

We are pleased to introduce to you the first book in the ROI Six Pack, which is part of the Measurement and Evaluation Series at Pfeiffer. These six books provide the latest tools, practical research, and how-to advice on measuring return on investment (ROI) in a variety of programs. This book offers an overview of the ROI Methodology.

The term *return on investment* summons a variety of images, ideas, concerns, and even fears. Some professionals are frightened by the idea of evaluating ROI for learning and development, performance improvement, human resources, technology, quality, and marketing. They become anxious about how ROI may be interpreted and used. Professionals who are open to learning about the ROI Methodology and its benefits, however, view it as an opportunity, a challenge, and a tool for improving programs and solutions. Although some debate its appropriateness, others quietly and deliberately pursue ROI in a variety of settings—and achieve impressive results.

The ROI Methodology is not for everyone or for every organization. Some organizations lack the trust and support that ROI requires. The successful champion of the ROI Methodology must be willing to learn, change, and try new things, using ROI as a process improvement tool. Without this attitude and approach, it may be best not to try. *ROI Fundamentals* provides the information necessary for individuals to use ROI to their advantage and become an advocate for the ROI Methodology.

ROI is growing in prominence and popularity; many professionals, managers, and senior leaders are trying to decide whether it is right for their organization, particularly for nontraditional applications. They need information about ROI, so that they can make decisions based on fact. Barriers to the implementation of ROI do exist; many of them are real, others perceived. Either way, these barriers can be eliminated—and success achieved—with the ROI Methodology. In the last decade, through our work with ROI, we have observed some realities about ROI; knowing about these realities may help individuals decide whether the pursuit of the ROI Methodology is worth the effort. The realities presented here reflect the drivers behind these six books and illustrate some of the challenges that an advocate will face. The stage is set for training and performance improvement executives who can accept the realities and challenges of ROI and use it to reach their goals.

ROI Reality #1

Although the ROI Methodology can be implemented in many situations, several perceived issues inhibit its use. Although real barriers exist, most of the inhibitors are myths based on misunderstandings of the process and what it can achieve.

The ROI Methodology is a tool that currently enjoys widespread application; however, many individuals involved in ROI implementation attend ROI certification workshops with built-in resistance. Their participation is driven by senior management or by ultimatums from the top executive group. Their hesitancy is due, in part, to fear of the unknown and fear of what the results of an ROI evaluation will do, particularly if the resulting ROI is negative. Individuals are concerned that a negative ROI might bring an end to their programs or, worse, their job. This concern is often based on misunderstanding and lack of knowledge. A comment from the audience at a keynote presentation at the International Conference of the American Society for Training and Development underscores this concern: "I [a store manager] transferred to the training and development function to escape numbers and, ultimately, the accountability that goes along with them. Now, it looks like I have to face the same type of numbers here." The comment drew a round of applause and also illustrates another fear—the fear of anything to do with numbers. The reality is that numbers are involved, but it is not necessary to be a statistician to apply or benefit from ROI. The perception that one needs a graduate degree in program evaluation is not at all correct and presents one of many unwarranted claims against the use of ROI.

ROI Fundamentals, the first book in the ROI Six Pack, explores and dispels many of the myths about ROI that challenge its use. Misconceptions act as barriers, deterring application and implementation of the ROI Methodology. Although very real barriers do exist—for example, barriers of time, cost, and skill—the benefits of the methodology far outweigh the investment.

ROI Reality #2

> Lack of information about ROI or, worse, misinformation about ROI can send clients on a misdirected course. Prospective clients need more information on the benefits of and barriers to implementing ROI.

The ROI Six Pack was developed in response to clients' needs. Organizations pursuing ROI have asked for more detail on the business realities of ROI. They want to know up front the actual benefits and the expected payoff of using the ROI Methodology.

An understanding of what the ROI Methodology can achieve requires clarification of the issues, terms, and concepts that are basic to understanding the process. *ROI Fundamentals* addresses this need by providing information that will help readers

- Increase their understanding of the ROI Methodology, its concept, and its assumptions.

- Identify who is using the ROI Methodology, why they are using it, and for what types of applications they are using it. It is important to see who is—and who is not—embracing this process improvement tool.

- Make a decision about ROI. This is a critical issue! Most people explore the ROI Methodology with these questions: "Is this right for us? Is this needed in our organization at this time?" *ROI Fundamentals* provides the information needed to answer these questions.

- Increase their understanding of how the ROI Methodology can add value to an organization.

- Dispel the inhibiting myths about ROI that can prevent successful implementation.

- Plot their next steps.

This first book in the Six Pack is not a detailed reference for the ROI Methodology; the other five books in this series detail each step in the process, providing resources for application and implementation. Instead, *ROI Fundamentals* is about understanding and making sense of the ROI Methodology from a business perspective.

ROI Reality #3

Using ROI effectively will require individuals and organizations to build new skills and learn processes.

Unfortunately, preparation for most of today's professionals in learning and development, human resources, quality, technology, and marketing has not involved learning how to conduct measurement and evaluations. Few courses in college degree programs cover appropriate analytical techniques, and measurement and evaluation is rarely required. Therefore, individuals may be unprepared to conduct ROI analyses. The ROI Six Pack is designed specifically to address this need, using simple, straightforward language. The steps, tasks, processes, and issues involved in calculating ROI are fully explored in these six books.

ROI Reality #4

The ROI Methodology is being implemented globally in all types of organizations and for all types of programs. Many training and development, organizational development, performance improvement, and human resources professionals are using the ROI Methodology to radically change the way they design, develop, and deliver programs and solutions.

The number of applications of the ROI Methodology has grown significantly; hundreds of organizations in different settings across the globe now use it. The ROI Methodology has been used in practically every country. Through our international associates, we have been involved in its implementation in organizations in almost fifty countries. The ROI Methodology is proving to be a valuable performance tool, and the number of converts is rapidly growing.

Growth in the application of the ROI Methodology cuts across all types of organizations and industries. When one major organization in an industry begins using it, others become interested. For example, the three largest package delivery companies in the world have implemented the ROI Methodology, partly because their peers were using it. For the same reason, almost all major telecommunications companies in the United States have implemented this methodology.

The ROI Methodology has also moved into different organizational sectors. At first, it was used almost exclusively in the manufacturing sector—the logical birthplace of any process improvement. It quickly moved to the service sector, then to nonprofit organizations, and on to government organizations. Now, it is being applied in the education sector, where schools and universities are using ROI to show the value of their programs.

Whereas initially the ROI Methodology was employed to show the impact of training in cooperative education programs, it quickly spread to all types of programs, from highly technical programs to long-term executive development. The ROI Methodology has been successfully applied in coaching and management development programs—for example, business coaching, mentoring, and career development. Human resources programs—such as orientation, compensation systems, recruiting strategies, employee relation initiatives, and retention solutions—have also been successfully evaluated using the ROI Methodology. Applications have moved beyond the human resources and learning and performance improvement arena to include systems, technology, change, quality, meetings and events, marketing, and a variety of public sector and social programs.

Finally, the number of individuals who have attended formal training in the ROI Methodology continues to grow rapidly. Over 20,000 specialists and managers have attended almost 1,000 ROI two-day workshops conducted in major cities throughout the world. Over 5,000 individuals have been prepared to implement the methodology internally through an ROI certification process.

ROI Reality #5

A new breed of performance improvement executive is achieving success with the ROI Methodology. Operating with a business mindset, such executives are using the methodology to prove the value of their programs. They are becoming business partners in the organization.

The good news is that changes are being made and success achieved. A new breed of performance improvement executive is managing training and development, performance improvement, and human resources functions. The new executives bring a business mindset to the table. They want to operate their function as an important business enterprise, as a major contributor that adds value to the business, and they use the ROI Methodology to support their cause.

In implementing the ROI Methodology, the new executives are choosing to be proactive instead of reactive. They realize that they must take the lead and initiate change or it will not happen. ROI is being recognized as a necessary tool. In any functional part of a business, performance must be validated in order to be recognized as a contributor.

Finally, the new breed of performance improvement executive accepts the challenging aspects of implementing the ROI Methodology. It is difficult to apply the process to all the different situations, scenarios, and environments in which it must work in order to be a useful tool. The new executives understand that it will take time to change their practices and implement the methodology.

ROI Reality #6

Sooner or later, every function will face a need for increased accountability and will have to address ROI. For some, the time is now. For others, the time may come later, but the need will eventually surface.

Let's face it, even in organizations in which tradition offers plentiful financial endowment, stakeholder questions arise, such as

• Did the program make a difference?

• Was it worth the investment?

- Did we make or save more than we spent on the project?

- Could another program or even another department achieve better results at less cost?

Resources are limited. A tool is needed that allows decision makers to base their decisions about investments on a single common measure. That measure is ROI, and although it is not new, in many organizations its use is expanding across functions. Ultimately, the use of ROI across an organization will allow decision makers to compare functional as well as programmatic contributions, based on a common metric and using a standard process.

ROI Fundamentals details the important influences responsible for the growth of the ROI Methodology. These influences include the following:

- Global economic forces that make it necessary for all segments of an organization to show the payoff of all types of solutions and programs. Every function must make a contribution.

- ROI's position as the ultimate level of evaluation, in which the cost of the solution is compared with the monetary benefits of the solution. Even though other levels of evaluation are important, nothing tells the story quite like ROI, particularly for sponsors and clients who require a monetary payback.

- ROI's familiarity among managers, particularly those who have a business degree. They see ROI as an important accountability tool. They have seen it applied in the evaluation of capital expenditures and welcome its use in evaluation of performance initiatives. They realize that ROI is not a fad; it is a proven technique that will be here for years to come.

- Top executives' requirement that the ROI of new (and existing) programs be measured. Previously, executives hesitated to ask for ROI because they didn't realize it could be done. In some situations, they were told that it is impossible to measure ROI for certain projects or programs. Now, they are learning that this level of evaluation can be done, so they are requiring it.

Some people still believe that ROI is an unrealistic approach to measuring value for learning and development, performance improvement, human resources, quality, and other programs. In reality, the ROI Methodology presented in this book provides data that are important to all stakeholders and dispels the myths and mysteries about measuring value for program investments.

A Brief Description of the ROI Methodology

The ROI Methodology is represented by the basic model shown in Figure 1.1. This process model provides a systematic approach to ROI calculations; a potentially complicated process is simplified by breaking it into sequential steps. This step-by-step approach keeps the process manageable so that users can tackle one issue at a time. Applying the model also provides consistency from one ROI calculation to another. This chapter provides a brief description of the ROI Methodology and how it fits into a comprehensive process.

Evaluation Levels: A Beginning Point

The ROI Methodology collects and processes up to five levels of evaluation results. The process also considers what is referred to as Level 0, the initial data or inputs, which represent activities and investment associated with a program or project. Each level represents a different category of data; each category of data answers questions asked by various stakeholders.

For example, Level 0, Inputs and Indicators, represents the various inputs of the project or program. These data are collected for all programs; they include costs, efficiencies, duration (in hours or days), participants, and topics. These data are input only and do not necessarily correspond to the results; they merely represent

Figure 1.1. The ROI Process Model

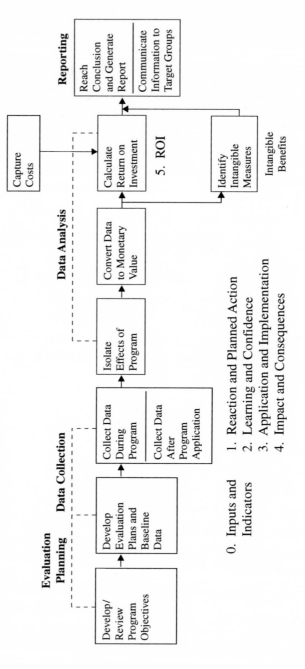

activity. Specific questions answered by data categorized at Level 0 include

- What steps have been taken to implement the program?
- How many people are involved in the program?
- Who was involved in the program?
- How much time has been spent on the program?
- What did the program cost the organization?

Level 1, Reaction and Planned Action, represents reaction from participants as well as actions planned as a result of the program. This level of evaluation is the first level that represents results—results from the perspective of participants. Almost all organizations evaluate at Level 1, usually with a generic end-of-program questionnaire. Specific questions answered by data collected at this level include

- Was the program delivered successfully?
- Was the content relevant to participants' current work?
- Was the content important to participants' current jobs?
- Do the participants intend to apply what they learned?
- Did the content represent new information?
- Will participants recommend the program to others?

While this level of evaluation is important as a customer satisfaction measure, a favorable reaction does not ensure that participants have learned new skills or knowledge.

At Level 2, Learning and Confidence, measurements focus on what participants learned during the program; learning is assessed through self-assessments, checklists, role plays, simulations, group evaluations, or other tools. A learning check is helpful to ensure that participants have absorbed the desired content and messages and know how to use or apply them properly. This level may also measure the number of new professional contacts made and the extent to which existing contacts were strengthened through networking that occurred during program implementation. Specific questions that are answered with Level 2 data include

- Do the participants "get it"?

- Do participants know what to do?

- Do participants know how to do it?

- Have participants' attitudes changed so that they are prepared to change behaviors or processes?

- Are participants confident in applying their newly acquired skills, knowledge, or information?

It is important to remember, however, that a positive learning measure is no guarantee that the learning or contacts acquired will actually be used.

At Level 3, Application and Implementation, a variety of follow-up methods are used to determine whether participants have applied what they learned. Completion of action items, behavior change, use of skills, and follow-up with contacts are important measures at Level 3. Questions answered by Level 3 data include

- Are participants applying their newly acquired knowledge, skills, or information?

- Are participants applying their newly acquired knowledge, skills, or information at the level of frequency expected?

- If participants are applying their newly acquired knowledge, skills, or information, what is supporting them?

- If they are not, why not?

While Level 3 evaluations are important to gauge the success of the application, they still do not guarantee that a positive impact will occur in the individual or the organization.

Level 4, Impact and Consequences, represents the actual results, or outcomes, achieved by participants as they successfully apply the content, messages, or contacts. Typical Level 4 measures include output, sales, quality, costs, time, and customer satisfaction. An important step taken during Level 4 data collection and analysis is isolating the impact of the program on these measures. Specific questions answered with Level 4 data include

- How does the application of newly acquired knowledge, skills, or information affect output, quality, cost, time, job satisfaction, employee satisfaction, or work habits?

- How does an organization know whether the program caused the impact?

Although the program may produce a measurable business impact, a concern may still exist that the program costs too much.

At Level 5, Return on Investment—the ultimate level of evaluation—the program's monetary benefits are compared with the program's costs. Although ROI can be expressed in several ways, it is usually presented as a percentage or benefit-cost ratio. The evaluation chain is not complete until the Level 5 evaluation is conducted. Here, the analysis should answer the most fundamental question: Do program benefits exceed program costs?

Table 1.1 summarizes the evaluation levels and the measures developed at each level. Readers should consider each level and

Table 1.1. Measurement at Each Level of Evaluation

Level	Measurement Category	Current Status in Your Organization	Evaluation Target for Most Organizations	Comments
0	**Inputs and Indicators** Measures inputs into programs, including the number of programs, participants, audience, costs, and efficiencies	100%	100%	This is being accomplished now.
1	**Reaction and Planned Action** Measures reaction to and satisfaction with the experience, ambience, content, and value of the program, as well as planned action after the program		100%	Most organizations evaluate 100% of programs at this level but need to focus more on content and planned action.
2	**Learning and Confidence** Measures what participants have learned in the program—information, knowledge, skills, or contacts (take-aways from the program)		80–90%	Simple learning measures can be integrated into the data collection process at Level 1.

3 Application and Implementation

Measures progress after the program—the use of information, knowledge, skills, or contacts

15–30%

Progress has been made, but more follow-up measures are needed.

4 Impact and Consequences

Measures changes in business impact variables (such as output, quality, time, or cost) linked to the program

10%

The link between the program and business impact is analyzed for select programs.

5 Return on Investment

Compares the monetary benefits of the business impact measures to the costs of the program

5%

The ultimate evaluation.

note the percentage of programs within their organization that are evaluated at each level. They should compare the current status of their evaluations with the targeted percentages in the table. These targets were developed on the basis of the evaluation practices of organizations currently implementing the ROI Methodology. As shown, not all programs should be evaluated at each level. Selecting programs to be evaluated at the higher levels depends on a variety of factors, including

- Purpose of evaluation

- Need for the program

- Program profile

- Stakeholders' needs

Selecting Programs for ROI Evaluation

Evaluation at Levels 4 and 5 is reserved for programs that are
  - Expensive
  - High-profile
  - Offered to a large audience
  - Linked to business objectives and strategy
  - Of interest to senior management

Even though data at the lower levels of evaluation do not necessarily predict success at the higher levels, data must be collected at the lower levels when evaluating at the higher levels. As participants take part in a program and react positively to it, acquiring knowledge, then applying that knowledge, business impact will occur as long as what was presented was needed and the right audience was targeted. If the business impact is as planned and program costs are less than the monetary benefits of program results, a positive

ROI will occur. This chain of impact provides the complete story of program success. Data important to all stakeholders are developed; together, these data can explain why the ROI is what it is and how it can be improved for future program implementations.

From the client's perspective, the value of information increases as evaluation moves up the chain of impact. The ROI Methodology is a client-centered process, meeting the data needs of the individuals who initiate, approve, and sponsor programs. Placing the client at the center of the evaluation process is consistent with the practices of benchmarking forum members of the American Society for Training and Development (ASTD) (Van Buren, 2002) and the best practices of corporate universities as identified in a study conducted by the American Productivity and Quality Center (Phillips, 2000).

Evaluation Planning

Planning is a critical phase in the ROI Methodology. A solid evaluation plan will foster successful execution as well as capture client buy-in before results are rendered. Several issues must be addressed when developing the evaluation plan for an ROI impact study. Five specific elements are important to evaluation success:

1. The evaluation purpose should be considered prior to developing the evaluation plan because the purpose will determine the scope of the evaluation, the types of instruments used, and the types of data collected.

2. The feasibility of a Level 4 or 5 evaluation should be examined. Feasibility is determined not only by the type of program undergoing evaluation but also by resources and time constraints.

3. It is imperative that objectives for different levels of evaluation be developed. Program objectives position the program for success as well as give direction to the evaluation.

4. Sources of data are an important consideration. While program participants will be the primary source of data in most cases, including other sources is also important to provide a balanced perspective and add credibility.

5. The timing of data collection is another consideration. In some cases, pre-program measurements are taken to compare with post-program measures. In other cases, measures are taken at intervals throughout the program. Sometimes, pre-program measurements are not available but post-program follow-up measures are still taken.

To complete the planning process, three simple planning documents are developed: the data collection plan, the ROI analysis plan, and the project plan. These documents should be completed before the evaluation project is implemented (ideally, before the program is designed or developed). Appropriate up-front attention will save much time later when data are actually collected.

The data collection plan outlines the major elements and issues involved in collecting data for evaluation at Levels 1 through 4. A target ROI (Level 5) is also established during planning. Table 1.2 shows a completed data collection plan for a program on interactive sales skills. The three-day training program was designed for retail sales associates in the electronics department of a major store chain (Phillips and Phillips, 2001). An ROI calculation was planned for a pilot of three groups.

The ROI analysis plan is a continuation of the data collection plan. It captures information on several key items that are necessary to develop the actual ROI calculation, including techniques to isolate the effects of the program as well as convert Level 4 measures to units of money. Along with these elements, cost categories, intangible benefits, and communication targets are identified. Table 1.3 shows a completed ROI analysis plan for the interactive selling skills program.

Table 1.2. Sample Data Collection Plan

Program: Interactive Sales Training   **Responsibility:** P. Phillips   **Date:** _____

Level	Broad Program Objectives	Measures	Data Collection Method and Instruments	Data Sources	Timing	Responsibility
1	**REACTION AND PERCEIVED VALUE**					
	• Positive reaction— 4 out of 5	• A 1–5 rating on a composite of five measures	• Questionnaire	• Participant	• End of program (third day)	• Facilitator
	• Action items	• Yes or No				
2	**LEARNING**					
	• Learn to use five simple skills	• Pass or fail on skill practice	• Observation of skill practice by facilitator	• Facilitator	• Second day of program	• Facilitator

(Continued)

Table 1.2. Sample Data Collection Plan (*Continued*)

Level	Broad Program Objectives	Measures	Data Collection Method and Instruments	Data Sources	Timing	Responsibility
3	**APPLICATION AND IMPLEMENTATION**					
	• Initial use of five simple skills	• Verbal feedback	• Follow-up session	• Participant	• Three weeks after second day	• Facilitator
	• At least 50% of participants use all skills with every customer	• Fifth item checked on a 1–5 scale	• Follow-up questionnaire	• Participant	• Three months after program	• Store training coordinator
4	**BUSINESS IMPACT**					
	• Increase in sales	• Weekly average sales per sales associate	• Business performance monitoring	• Company records	• Three months after program	• Store training coordinator
5	**ROI**					
	• 50%					

Comments: The ROI objective was set at a high value because of the store sample size; the executives wanted convincing data.

Table 1.3. Sample ROI Analysis Plan

Program: Interactive Sales Training   **Responsibility:** P. Phillips   **Date:**

Data Items	Methods of Isolating the Effects of the Program	Methods of Converting Data	Cost Categories	Intangible Benefits	Communication Targets	Other Influences and Issues
• Weekly sales per associate	• Control group analysis • Participant estimate	• Direct conversion using profit contribution	• Facilitation fees • Program materials • Meals and refreshments • Facilities • Participant salaries and benefits • Cost of coordination • Evaluation	• Customer satisfaction • Employee satisfaction	• Program participants • Electronics department managers at targeted stores • Store managers at targeted stores • Senior store executives in district, region, headquarters • Training staff: instructors, coordinators, designers, and managers	• Must have job coverage during training • No communication with control group • Seasonal fluctuations should be avoided

The third plan that is developed in the evaluation planning phase is a project plan, which provides a description of the program and a timeline for the project, from planning of the evaluation to communication of the results. Exhibit 1.1 shows a sample project plan.

Collectively, these three planning documents provide the necessary direction for the ROI evaluation. Because most of the decisions about the evaluation process are made as these planning tools are developed, the remainder of the project becomes a systematic process of implementing the plan. Time allocated to this process will save precious time later.

Data Collection

Data collection is central to the ROI Methodology. Deciding how to collect the data, from whom to collect the data, and when to collect the data is fundamental to a successful ROI study. Both hard data (for example, output, quality, cost, and time data) and soft data (for example, job satisfaction and customer satisfaction) are collected, using a variety of methods:

- *Surveys* are administered to determine whether participants are satisfied with the program and to what degree, whether they have learned the desired skills and knowledge, and whether they have used various aspects of the program. Survey responses usually consist of perception or attitudinal data, often represented on a scale. Surveys are used to collect data at Levels 1, 2, and 3.

- *Questionnaires* are more detailed than surveys and can be used to uncover a variety of quantitative and qualitative data. Participants provide responses to

Exhibit 1.1. Project Plan

	FEB	MAR	APR	MAY	JUN	JUL	AUG	SEP
Decision to conduct ROI study	▓							
Evaluation planning complete	▓							
Instruments designed	▓							
Instruments pilot-tested		▓						
Data collected from Group A			▓					
Data collected from Group B				▓				
Data collected from Group C					▓			
Data tabulation, preliminary summary					▓			
Analysis conducted						▓		
Report written						▓		
Report printed						▓		
Results communicated							▓	
Improvements initiated							▓	
Implementation complete								▓

several types of open-ended and forced-response questions. Questionnaires can be used to capture data at Levels 1, 2, 3, and 4.

- *Tests* are conducted to measure changes in knowledge and skills (Level 2). A wide variety of methods are used, ranging from formal (criterion-referenced tests, norm-referenced tests, performance tests, simulations, and skill practices) to informal (facilitator assessment, self-assessment, and team assessment).

- On-the-job *observation* captures actual skill application and use. Observations are particularly useful in customer service training and are most effective when the observer is unnoticeable to the participant being observed. Observations are appropriate for collecting Level 3 data.

- *Interviews* are conducted with participants to determine the extent to which learning has been used on the job. Interviewers can probe to uncover specific applications. Interviews are most often used for collecting Level 3 data but can also be used to collect Level 1 and Level 2 data. Occasionally, interviews are used to collect Level 4 data.

- *Focus groups* are conducted to determine the degree to which a group of participants has applied the program to job situations. Focus groups are usually appropriate for collecting Level 3 data, but are also used in making the link between business impact and the program.

- *Action plans and program assignments* are developed by participants during the program and are implemented on the job after the program is completed. Follow-up on action plans and program assignments provides evidence of program success. Level 3 and Level 4 data can be collected using action plans.

- *Performance contracts* are developed by the participant, the participant's supervisor, and the facilitator. They all agree on job performance outcomes from the program. Performance contracts are appropriate for collecting both Level 3 and Level 4 data.

- *Business performance monitoring* is useful when performance records and operational data can be examined for improvement. This method is particularly useful for collecting Level 4 data.

Along with selecting the appropriate data collection method, consideration must be given to the source of data, which is primarily (but not always exclusively) the participant. Timing is a third consideration. Fundamental timing considerations include the time at which data are needed, the availability of data, and the availability of resources. These issues are covered in more detail in *Data Collection*, the second book of this series.

Isolation of Program Effects

An issue that is overlooked in most evaluations is how to isolate the effects of the program. In this step of the process, evaluation planners explore specific techniques for determining the amount of impact directly related to the program. Because many factors will affect performance data, this step is essential for increasing the accuracy and credibility of ROI calculations. The following techniques have been used by organizations to address this important issue.

- A *control group* arrangement is often used to isolate the impact of a specific program. One group participates in the program, while another similar group (the control group) does not participate. The difference in the performance of the two groups is attributed to the program. When properly set up and implemented, the control group arrangement is the most effective way to isolate the effects of a program or project.

- *Trend lines* are used to project the values of specific impact measures before the program is undertaken. The projection is compared with the actual data after the program is conducted, and the difference represents an estimate of the impact of the program. Under certain conditions, this technique can accurately isolate the program impact.

- When mathematical relationships between input and output measures are known, a *forecasting model* can be used to isolate the effects of a program. The impact measure is predicted by using the forecasting model with pre-program data. The actual performance of the measure, weeks or months after the program, is compared with the forecasted value. The results are an estimate of the impact.

- *Participants* estimate the amount of improvement that is related to the program. Participants are provided with the total amount of improvement, based on a comparison of pre- and post-program measurements, and are asked to indicate the percentage of the improvement that is related to the program.

- *Participants' supervisors* estimate the effect of the program on the impact measures. The supervisors are given the total amount of improvement and are asked to indicate the percentage that can be directly attributed to the program.

- *Senior management* estimates the impact of the program. In such cases, managers provide an estimate of how much of the improvement is related to the program. Although it may be inaccurate, having senior management involved in the process has some advantages.

- *Experts* provide estimates of the program's impact on the performance measure. Because the estimates are based on previous experience, the experts must be familiar with the type of program and the specific situation.

- When feasible, all *other influencing factors* are identified and their impact is estimated or calculated; the remaining unexplained improvement is attributed to the program.

- In some situations, *customers* provide input on the extent to which the program has influenced their decisions to use a product or service. Although this strategy has limited applications, it can be quite useful for isolating the effects of customer service and sales programs.

Collectively, these techniques provide a comprehensive set of tools to address the critical issue of isolating the effects of a program. The third book in this series, *Isolation of Results*, is devoted to this important step in the ROI Methodology.

Data Conversion

To calculate the return on investment, Level 4 impact data are converted to monetary values and compared with program costs. This step requires that a value be placed on each unit of data connected with the program. Many techniques for converting data to monetary values are available; which technique is appropriate depends on the type of data and the situation.

- *Output data* are converted to profit contribution or cost savings. When using this technique, output increases are converted to monetary values based on their unit contribution to profit or the unit of cost reduction. Standard values for these items are readily available in most organizations.

- The *cost of quality* is calculated, and quality improvements are converted directly to cost savings. Standard values for these items are available in many organizations.

- For programs in which employee time is saved, the *participants' wages and employee benefits* are used to develop a value for the time saved. Because a variety of programs focus on improving the time required to complete projects, processes, or daily activities, the value of time is an important issue. This is a standard formula in most organizations.

- *Historical costs*, developed from cost statements, are used when they are available for a specific measure. Organizational cost data thus establish the specific monetary costs saved or avoided by an improvement.

- When available, *internal and external experts* may be used to estimate the value of an improvement. In this situation, the credibility of the estimate hinges on the expertise and reputation of the experts themselves.

- *External databases* are sometimes available to estimate the value or cost of data items. Research, government, and industry databases can provide important information on these values. Although data are plentiful, the difficulty of this technique lies in finding a specific database related to the program or situation.

- *Participants* estimate the value of the data item. For this approach to be effective, participants must be capable of providing a value for the improvement.

- *Supervisors or managers* can provide estimates if they are both willing and able to assign values to the improvement. This approach is especially useful when the participants are not fully capable of providing this input or in situations in which supervisors need to confirm or adjust the participants' estimates. This approach is particularly helpful in establishing values for performance measures that are important to senior management.

- *Soft measures are linked mathematically to other measures* that are easier to measure and value. This approach is particularly helpful in establishing values for measures that are very difficult to convert to monetary values— for example, data related to intangibles such as customer satisfaction, employee satisfaction, conflict, or employee complaints.

- *Staff estimates* may be used to determine a value for an output data item. The estimates must be provided on an unbiased basis.

The data conversion step is absolutely necessary in order to determine the monetary benefits of a program. The process is challenging, particularly when soft data are involved, but it can be accomplished by methodically using one or more of the listed techniques. Because of the importance of assigning monetary values to impact data, the fourth book in this series, *Data Conversion*, is devoted to this step in the ROI Methodology, along with identifying intangible benefits.

Intangible Benefits

In addition to their tangible monetary benefits, most programs will have intangible nonmonetary benefits. The ROI calculation is based on converting both hard and soft data to monetary values. Intangible benefits are program benefits that individuals choose not to convert to monetary values. Intangible benefits often include such measures as

- Increased job satisfaction

- Increased employee engagement

- Improved teamwork

- Improved creativity

- Reduced complaints

- Reduced conflicts

During data analysis, every attempt is made to convert all data to monetary values. All hard data, such as those related to output, quality, and time, are converted to monetary values. The conversion of soft data is attempted for each data item. However, if the process used for conversion is too subjective or inaccurate, the resulting values lose credibility; in such cases, the data are listed as an intangible benefit, with an appropriate explanation. For some programs, intangible nonmonetary benefits are extremely valuable, carrying as much influence as the hard data items.

Program Costs

The second part of a benefit-cost analysis is the program costs. Tabulating costs involves monitoring or developing all the related costs of the program targeted for ROI evaluation. Among the cost components that should be included are

- The cost of the needs assessment (when conducted) prorated over the program's expected life

- The cost of designing and developing the program, possibly prorated over the program's expected life

- The cost of all program materials provided to each participant

- The cost of the instructor or facilitator, including preparation time as well as delivery time

- The cost of the facilities

- Travel, lodging, and meal costs of the participants, if applicable

- Salaries and employee benefits of the participants for the time that they are involved in the program

- Administrative and overhead costs of the functional unit, allocated in some convenient way

In addition, specific costs related to the needs assessment and evaluation should be included. The conservative approach is to include all these costs so that the total is fully loaded. Because of the importance of ascertaining program costs, the fifth book in the series, *Costs and ROI*, is devoted to this step, along with ROI calculation.

Return on Investment Calculation

The benefit-cost ratio (BCR) is calculated from the program benefits and costs. The benefit-cost ratio is the program benefits divided by the program costs. In formula form, it is written like this:

$$BCR = \frac{\text{Program Benefits}}{\text{Program Costs}}$$

The ROI for a program is the program's net benefits divided by the program's costs. (Net benefits are the program's benefits minus the program's costs.) Thus, in formula form, ROI is as follows:

$$ROI\ (\%) = \frac{\text{Net Program Benefits}}{\text{Program Costs}} \times 100$$

This is the same basic formula that is used in evaluating other investments, in which ROI is traditionally reported as earnings divided by investment. The fifth book in our series, *Costs and ROI*, provides more detail on ROI calculations.

Reporting

The final step in the ROI Methodology is reporting. Reporting often does not receive the attention and planning that is needed to ensure its success. This step involves developing appropriate information in impact studies and other brief reports. The heart of the step is the different techniques used to communicate to a wide variety of target audiences. In most ROI studies, several audiences are interested in and need the information. Careful planning in order to match the communication method with the audience is essential, to ensure that the message is understood and that appropriate actions follow. The sixth book in the ROI Six Pack, *Communication and Implementation*, is devoted to this critical step.

Case Study

Table 1.4 shows the results from a sample case study. The table includes all the elements described in this chapter. The All-Inclusive Workforce Program explored diversity issues and targeted both

Table 1.4. Case Study of Program Evaluation Using ROI Methodology

Sprint/Nextel

Program Title: Diversity

Target Group: Managers and employees

Solution: All-Inclusive Workforce Program (AIW)

Results:

Level 1: Reaction and Planned Action	*Level 2:* Learning and Confidence	*Level 3:* Application and Implementation	*Level 4:* Impact	*Level 5:* ROI	Intangible Benefits
Composite rating: 4.39 out of 5 (for six items)	Averaged 4.28 out of 5 (for learning on six objectives)	*Managers:* Support AIW (87%) Address problems (81%) Encourage staff (78%) *Employees:* Support AIW (65%) Identify differences (63%) Encourage staff (60%) 91% of managers successfully completed action plans	Attrition rate improvement = 9.77%	BCR: 2.6 ROI: 163%	Employee satisfaction Communication Cooperation Diversity mix Teamwork

Technique for Isolating the Effects of the Program: Manager's estimate, adjusted for error

Technique for Converting Data to Monetary Values: Standard cost item ($89,000 per turnover)

Fully Loaded Program Costs: $1,216,836

Source: Schmidt, 2003.

managers and employees. All six types of data were collected, including the actual ROI. This summary shows all the types of data and also addresses the issues of isolating the effects of the program, converting the data to monetary values, and monitoring the program costs.

Final Thoughts

This chapter presents the basic process for calculating the return on investment for programs or projects. The step-by-step process breaks the complicated problem of calculating ROI into simple, manageable tasks and steps. When the process is thoroughly planned, taking into consideration all potential strategies and techniques, it becomes manageable and achievable. The remaining chapters focus on the major elements of this model and on ways to implement it.

References

Phillips, J. J. *The Corporate University: Measuring the Impact of Learning.* Houston, Tex.: American Productivity and Quality Center, 2000.

Phillips, P. P., and Phillips, J. J. *In Action: Measuring Return on Investment.* Vol. 3. Alexandria, Va.: ASTD, 2001. (See the chapter titled "Measuring Return on Investment in Interactive Sales Training.")

Schmidt, L. *In Action: Implementing Training Scorecards.* Alexandria, Va.: ASTD, 2003.

Van Buren, M. E. *State of the Industry.* Alexandria, Va.: ASTD, 2002.

2

Why ROI?

M easuring ROI has earned a place among the critical issues in the fields of learning and development, human resources, technology, quality, and marketing. The topic appears routinely on the agendas of conferences and professional meetings. Journals and newsletters have been devoting increasing print space to articles about ROI. A professional organization has been developed to exchange information on ROI. At least a dozen books provide detailed coverage of the topic. Even top executives have increased their appetite for ROI information.

Measurement of ROI is a much-debated topic. Few business topics stir up emotions to the degree that the ROI issue does. Measuring ROI is characterized as flawed and inappropriate by some, while others describe it as the only answer to their accountability concerns. The truth lies somewhere in the middle. Understanding the drivers of the ROI Methodology and its inherent weaknesses and advantages makes it possible to take a rational approach to the issue and implement an appropriate mix of evaluation strategies that include measuring ROI. This chapter presents the basic issues and trends in ROI measurement.

Although interest in the topic has grown and much progress has been made, ROI is still an issue that challenges even the most sophisticated and progressive organizations. While some professionals argue that calculating ROI is too difficult, others quietly and deliberately develop measures and routinely calculate ROI. The latter group is gaining support from senior management teams. Regardless of the position one takes on the issue, the reasons for measuring ROI are clear. Almost all professionals in the fields mentioned earlier share a concern that they must eventually show a return on investments made in their major programs. If they do not, funds may be reduced or their department or functional unit may not be able to maintain or enhance its present status and influence within the organization.

The measurement dilemma at the heart of the ROI process is a source of frustration for many senior executives. Executives realize that major processes such as learning, human resources, technology, and marketing are necessary when organizations experience significant growth or increased competition. These processes are also important during business restructuring and rapid change. Executives intuitively feel that these processes add value and logically conclude that they pay off in terms of important bottom-line measures such as productivity improvement, quality enhancement, cost reduction, and time saved, as well as enhanced customer satisfaction, improved morale, and improved teamwork. Yet executives become frustrated with the lack of evidence that shows the actual contributions of initiatives in the fields in which ROI measurement is difficult. The ROI Methodology represents the most promising way to achieve such accountability through a logical, rational approach; and this methodology is fully described in the Measurement and Evaluation Series.

Progress and Status of ROI

This chapter begins with a review of global trends in the use of ROI, a look at the overall progress that has been made in ROI evaluations, and the current status of ROI Methodology use. The status varies from field to field. In determining the economic benefit of public projects, cost-benefit analysis has been used for centuries.

The same is true for the use of ROI in accounting and finance. In learning and development, ROI evaluations are becoming routine in most organizations. In other fields, such as meetings and events, ROI evaluations are just starting to become frequently used tools for professionals.

Global Trends in Measurement

A few trends in measurement and evaluation in organizations in both the private and public sectors have been observed on a global basis. The following measurement trends have been identified in our research and are slowly evolving across organizations and cultures in nearly fifty countries. Collectively, these trends have an important impact on the way accountability issues are being addressed.

- No longer thought of as an add-on activity, evaluation is an integral part of the design, development, delivery, and implementation of programs.

- Organizations are shifting from a reactive approach to a more proactive approach, addressing evaluation early in the cycle.

- Measurement and evaluation processes are systematic and methodical, and they are often built into the delivery process, such as by the use of action plans.

- Technology is significantly enhancing the measurement and evaluation process, enabling large amounts of data to be collected, processed, analyzed, and integrated across programs.

- Evaluation planning is becoming a critical part of the measurement and evaluation cycle because only a carefully planned implementation will be successful.

- The implementation of a comprehensive measurement and evaluation process usually leads to increased emphasis on the initial needs analysis.

- Organizations without a comprehensive measurement and evaluation process have often reduced or eliminated their program budgets.

- Organizations with comprehensive measurement and evaluation have increased their program budgets.

- Use of ROI is emerging as an essential part of the measurement and evaluation process. ROI is a familiar term and concept for most executives; therefore they understand ROI and appreciate its usefulness.

- Many examples of successful ROI applications are available.

- A comprehensive measurement and evaluation process, including measurement of ROI, can be implemented for about 3 or 5 percent of the direct program budget.

ROI Applications Across Fields and Sectors

The ROI Methodology described in this book had its beginnings in the 1970s when it was applied to a cooperative education program. Since then, it has been developed, modified, and refined into the process described here, and it has been applied in many types of situations and sectors.

Exhibit 2.1 shows how the process has evolved in different applications and fields. Manufacturing and service sectors were early adopters of the ROI Methodology. In the health care arena, applications evolved as the industry sought ways to improve educational services, human resources, quality, risk management, and case management. Nonprofit applications emerged as nonprofit organizations pursued ways to reduce costs and generate efficiencies. Finally, applications appeared in a variety of government organizations. Public sector implementation has increased in recent years. An outgrowth of public sector applications is the use of the ROI Methodology in academia, where it is now being applied not only to internal processes but to continuing education and graduate programs as well. The ROI Methodology is spreading to all types of organizations, settings, and professional fields. The specific types of program applications vary; current applications represent a full range of programs from learning and development, education, human resources, quality, marketing, change, and technology. Cases have been published in all of these areas. The process is flexible, versatile, and adaptable to almost any type of setting and environment.

Exhibit 2.1. ROI Applications

- Human resources, human capital
- Learning and development, performance improvement
- Technology, information technology systems
- Meetings and events
- Sales, marketing
- Public relations, community affairs, government relations
- Project management solutions
- Quality, Six Sigma
- Operations, methods, engineering
- Research and development, innovation
- Finance, compliance
- Logistics, distribution, supply chain
- Public policy initiatives
- Social programs
- Charitable projects
- Community and faith-based initiatives

Growth of ROI as a Conference Topic

Sometimes, the best way to judge interest in a topic or trend is to observe the conferences offered on the subject. The International Quality and Productivity Center routinely offers conferences on ROI—sometimes as many as four or five per year—not only in the United States but also in Europe, Southeast Asia, and Australia. These conferences are designed to explore issues involving ROI, particularly its implementation and use.

The ROI Network has offered conferences each year for a decade. The American Productivity and Quality Center has also offered conferences on ROI. The Institute for Industrial Relations, based in Europe, has offered conferences that included topics on ROI in Europe, Canada, and the United States.

Training magazine's annual conference, the Training Director's Forum; ASTD; and the International Society for Performance Improvement (ISPI), and other associations routinely feature ROI as an important agenda topic.

Global Expansion of ROI Applications

Measuring ROI is becoming a truly global issue. Organizations from all over the world are concerned about accountability and are exploring techniques to measure the results of various programs. In a survey of thirty-five members of the International Federation of Training and Development Organizations, measuring ROI was consistently rated the hottest topic. Whether an economy is mature or developing, accountability remains a critical issue.

Many professional associations in different countries have offered workshops, seminars, and dedicated conferences on issues of measurement, including measurement of ROI. Some associations have sponsored individual workshops on ROI. Formal presentations on ROI have been made in over fifty countries and implementation organized and coordinated in at least forty countries.

Table 2.1. Paradigm Shift Toward Accountability in Programs and Projects

Characteristics of an Activity-Based Process	Characteristics of a Results-Based Process
• No business need for the program	• Program linked to specific business needs
• No assessment of performance issues	• Assessment of performance effectiveness
• No specific measurable objectives for application and impact	• Specific objectives defined for application and impact
• No effort to prepare program participants to achieve results	• Results expectations communicated to participants
• No effort to prepare the work environment to support application	• Environment prepared to support application of the program
• No efforts to build partnerships with key managers	• Partnerships established with key managers and clients
• No measurement of results or cost-benefit analysis	• Measurement of results and cost-benefit analysis
• Input-focused planning and reporting	• Output-focused planning and reporting

The Move from Activity to Results

The widespread growth of interest in ROI applications underscores the need for programs to shift from an activity-based process to a results-based process. Table 2.1 depicts the paradigm shift that has occurred in recent years, dramatically affecting accountability in all types of programs. Organizations have moved from activity to a focus on bottom-line results. The shift has often occurred because of the trends described earlier in this chapter. In some cases, the shift has occurred because progressive departments have recognized the need to measure ROI and have been persistent in making progress on the issue.

ROI Is Here to Stay

One thing in the ROI debate is certain: ROI measurement is not a fad. As long as investment payoff and accountability for program expenditures are required, ROI will be used to evaluate major investments.

A fad is a new idea or approach or a new spin on an old approach. ROI has been used for centuries. The seventy-fifth anniversary issue of the *Harvard Business Review* (HBR) traced the tools used to measure results in organizations (Sibbet, 1997). In the early issues of HBR, during the 1920s, ROI was reported as an emerging tool for assigning a value to the payoff of investments.

Today, hundreds of organizations are routinely developing ROI calculations for their programs. Given this increased adoption and use, it appears that the ROI Methodology as an accountability tool is here to stay.

Its status and implementation have grown at a high rate. The number of organizations and individuals involved with the process underscores the magnitude of ROI implementation. Exhibit 2.2 presents a summary of the ROI Methodology's current status. With this much evidence of growing interest, the ROI Methodology appears well on its way to becoming a standard tool for program evaluation.

Why ROI?

There are good reasons why ROI has gained acceptance as a business tool. Although the viewpoints and explanations may vary, some things are very clear. The key reasons are outlined in this section.

Exhibit 2.2. ROI by the Numbers: A Summary of the Current Status of the ROI Methodology

- The ROI Methodology has been refined over twenty-five years.
- The ROI Methodology has been adopted by hundreds of organizations in manufacturing, service, nonprofit, and government settings.
- Thousands of studies using the ROI Methodology are developed each year.
- Over one hundred case studies have been published on the ROI Methodology.
- Almost five thousand individuals have been certified to implement the ROI Methodology in their organizations.
- Organizations in forty countries have implemented the ROI Methodology.
- Two dozen books have been developed to support the process of implementing the ROI Methodology.
- A professional network has been formed to share information on the ROI Methodology.
- The ROI Methodology can be implemented for 3 to 5 percent of a program or project budget.

Increased Budgets

Most program budgets have continued to grow year after year. In almost any of the functional areas of human resources, quality, technology, and marketing, the cumulative average growth rate of expenditures in the last decade is greater than the changes in the producer price index.

As organizations recognize the importance and necessity of these functional areas, budgets continue to increase annually in organizations, industries, and even entire countries. Many organizations and countries see these expenditures as investments instead of costs. Consequently, senior managers are willing to invest because they anticipate a payoff for their investments. As expenditures grow, accountability becomes more critical. A growing budget creates a larger target for internal critics, often prompting the development of an ROI evaluation process. The function, department, or process showing the most value will likely receive the largest budget increase.

The Ultimate Level of Evaluation

Table 1.1, in Chapter One, shows the five-level framework used in this book. The framework categorizes program results as follows:

- Level 1, Reaction and Planned Action

- Level 2, Learning and Confidence

- Level 3, Application and Implementation

- Level 4, Impact and Consequences

- Level 5, ROI

While data at all levels are important, Level 5, ROI, is the ultimate level. It is ROI that allows projects and programs across the organization to be compared according to common criteria. It is the ROI calculation that reports not only the benefits of a program but also how those benefits compare with the investment that was made to achieve them.

Change, Quality, and Reengineering

ROI applications have increased because of the growing interest in a variety of organizational improvement, quality, and change programs, which have dominated organizations, particularly in North America, Europe, and Asia. In their zeal for improvement, organizations have embraced almost any trend that appeared on the horizon. Unfortunately, many of these change efforts have not been successful and have turned out to be passing fads. Implementation of the ROI Methodology requires a thorough needs assessment and significant planning before a program is implemented. If these two elements are in place, passing fads, which are usually doomed to failure, can be avoided. With the ROI Methodology in place, a new change program that does not produce results will soon be exposed. Management will be aware of it early, and as a result, adjustments can be made.

Total quality management, continuous process improvement, and Six Sigma have brought increased attention to measurement issues. Today, organizations measure processes and outputs that were not previously measured, monitored, or reported. This focus has placed increased pressure on all functions to develop measures of program success.

Restructuring and reengineering initiatives and the threat of outsourcing have caused executives to focus more directly on bottom-line issues. Many processes have been reengineered to align programs more closely with business needs and to obtain maximum efficiencies in the project cycle. These change processes have brought increased attention to evaluation issues and have resulted in measurements of the contribution of specific programs, including ROI.

Business Mindset of Support Managers

The business management mindset of many staff and support managers causes them to place more emphasis on economic issues within their function. Today's managers are more aware of bottom-line issues in their organization and more knowledgeable about operational and financial concerns. These new, more enlightened managers often take a business approach to programs and measure ROI as part of their strategy.

ROI is a familiar concept for business managers, especially those with business administration and management degrees. They have studied ROI applications in their academic courses, using ROI to evaluate the decision to purchase equipment, build a new facility, or buy a new company. Consequently, they understand ROI and appreciate the benefits of applying the ROI Methodology to the evaluation of programs and projects.

The Trend Toward Accountability

A persistent trend toward accountability has occurred in organizations everywhere. Every support function now tries to show its worth by documenting the value that it adds to the organization. Given the emphasis on accountability, all functions must provide evidence of their contributions to their organization.

The trend toward accountability has resulted in a variety of measurement processes (shown in Figure 2.1), sometimes leaving potential users of the processes extremely confused. Amid the confusion, many organizations have migrated to the proven acceptance of ROI. Used for hundreds of years, ROI has, for

Figure 2.1. A Variety of Measurement Possibilities

the reasons outlined here, become a preferred choice for practitioners who need to demonstrate the monetary payoff of their programs.

Top Executive Requirements

ROI is drawing increased interest in the executive suite. Top executives who have watched their budgets continue to grow without appropriate accountability measures have become frustrated. In response, they have turned to ROI. Consequently, top executives are now demanding ROI calculations from departments and functions that previously were not required to provide them. For years, support managers convinced top executives that the monetary contribution of their functions couldn't be measured. Now, however, many executives are aware that it can be and is being measured in other organizations, and therefore they are demanding the same accountability from their own support managers.

The topic of ROI has been covered in a wide range of publications, including *Fortune, USA Today, Business Week, Harvard Business Review, The Wall Street Journal,* and the *Financial Times.* Executives seem to have a never-ending desire to explore applications of ROI. Even in Europe, Africa, and Asia, it is not unusual for the majority of participants in an ROI workshop to attend because their top executives require it.

Concerns About Using ROI

Although much progress has been made, many professionals and their managers still have concerns about the use of ROI. The mere presence of the process can create a dilemma for many organizations. When an organization embraces the ROI concept and implements the methodology, the management team usually anxiously waits for results, only to be disappointed when they are not readily available. For an ROI process to be useful, many issues—such as feasibility, simplicity, credibility, and soundness—must be balanced.

In addition, in order for the ROI process to be successfully used and accepted, it must satisfy three major audiences:

- Practitioners who design, develop, and deliver programs

- Senior managers, sponsors, and clients who initiate and support programs

- Researchers who need a credible process

Practitioners

For years, many practitioners and professionals have assumed that ROI for their particular unit could not be measured. When they examined a typical ROI measurement process, they found long formulas, complicated equations, and complex models that made the process appear too confusing. Given this perceived complexity, managers envisioned that huge efforts would be required for data collection and analysis and, more important, that high costs would be necessary to make the process successful. In light of these concerns, practitioners seek an ROI measurement process that is simple and easy to understand so that they can easily implement its steps and strategies. They also need a process that will not take an excessive period of time to implement and will not consume too much precious staff time. Finally, practitioners need a process that is affordable. Because they are competing for financial resources, they need a process that will require only a small portion of their budgets. In summary, the ROI measurement process, from the practitioner's perspective, must be user-friendly, time-saving, and cost-efficient.

Senior Managers, Sponsors, and Clients

Managers who must approve budgets, request programs, or live with the results of programs have a strong interest in developing ROI measurements. They want a process that provides quantifiable results, using a measure similar to the ROI formula applied to other types of investments. Senior managers have a never-ending desire to boil results down to an ROI calculation, reflected as a percentage.

And like practitioners, they want a process that is simple and easy to understand. The assumptions made in the calculations and the methodology used should reflect their point of reference, background, and level of understanding. They do not want or need a string of formulas, charts, and complicated models. Instead, they need a process that they can explain to others, if necessary. More important, they need a process with which they can identify, one that is sound and realistic and that earns their confidence.

Researchers

Finally, researchers will support only a process that measures up to close examination. Researchers usually insist that models, formulas, assumptions, and theories be sound and based on commonly accepted practices. The process must also produce accurate values and consistent outcomes. If estimates are necessary, researchers want the most accuracy possible within the constraints of the situation, realizing that adjustments must be made when there is uncertainty in the process.

Thus, the challenge is to develop a process of ROI measurement that will satisfy researchers and please practitioners and senior managers at the same time.

Criteria for an Effective ROI Process

To satisfy the needs of the three critical groups—practitioners, senior managers, and researchers—the process of measuring ROI must meet several requirements. Eleven essential criteria for an effective ROI process are described in this section.

1. The ROI process must be *simple*—void of complex formulas, lengthy equations, and complicated methodologies. Most ROI evaluation attempts fail to meet this requirement. Some ROI models have become too complex to understand and use because they attempt to obtain statistical perfection and use too many theories. Consequently, they have not been implemented.

2. The ROI process must be *economical* and easy to implement. The process should become a routine part of project development without requiring significant additional resources. Selecting sample program groups for ROI evaluations and early planning for ROI measurement are often necessary in order to make progress without adding staff.

3. The assumptions, methodology, and techniques must be *credible*. Logical, methodical steps are needed in order to earn the respect of practitioners, senior managers, and researchers. This requires a practical approach to the process.

4. From a researcher's perspective, the ROI process must be *theoretically sound* and based on generally accepted practices. Unfortunately, this requirement can lead to an extensive, complicated process. Ideally, the process will strike a balance between a practical, sensible approach and a sound theoretical basis. This may be one of the toughest challenges for those who wish to develop a model for measuring ROI.

5. The ROI process must *account for factors other than the program being evaluated* that may also have influenced output variables. Isolating the influence of the program or project, an issue that is often overlooked, is necessary to build the credibility and accuracy of the process. The ROI process should pinpoint the contribution of the program as opposed to other influences.

6. The ROI process must be *appropriate for a variety of programs*. Some models apply to only a small number of programs, such as sales or productivity training. Ideally, the process should be applicable to all types of programs.

7. The ROI process must have the *flexibility* to be applied on a pre-program basis as well as a post-program basis. In some situations, an estimate of the ROI is required before the program is developed. Ideally, practitioners should be able to adjust the process for a range of potential time frames.

8. The ROI process must be *applicable to all types of data*—hard data, which typically represent output, quality, costs, and time, as well as soft data, which represent less tangible concepts, such as job satisfaction and customer satisfaction.

9. The ROI process must *include the costs of the program*. The ultimate level of evaluation involves comparing benefits with costs. Although the term *ROI* has been loosely used to express any benefit of a program or project, an acceptable ROI formula must include costs. Omitting or underestimating the costs will destroy the credibility of the ROI values.

10. The actual calculation must use an *acceptable ROI formula*. This formula is often the benefit-cost ratio or the ROI calculation, expressed as a percentage. These formulas compare the actual expenditures for a project with the monetary benefits driven by the project. Although other financial terms may be substituted, using a standard financial calculation in the ROI process is important.

11. Finally, the ROI process must have a *successful track record* in a variety of applications. In far too many situations, models are created but never successfully applied. An effective ROI process should withstand the wear and tear of implementation and get the expected results.

We consider these criteria to be essential; thus, an ROI methodology should meet most if not all of these criteria. Unfortunately, most ROI processes do not. The good news is that the ROI Methodology presented in this book meets all of them.

Barriers to ROI Implementation

Although progress has been made in implementation of the ROI Methodology, barriers may inhibit its implementation. Some of these barriers are real, and others are myths based on misperceptions. Each barrier is briefly described in this section.

Financial and Time Costs

The ROI Methodology will add some cost and time to program evaluations, although the added amount will not be excessive. This barrier alone may stop many ROI implementations early in the process. However, a comprehensive ROI process can be implemented for only 3 to 5 percent of a unit's overall budget, and the additional investment in ROI could be offset by the positive results achieved from the programs or the elimination of unproductive or unprofitable programs.

Lack of Staff Skills and Orientation

Many professional staff members do not understand ROI, nor do they have the basic skills necessary to apply the methodology within the scope of their responsibilities. Measurement and evaluation are not usually part of the preparation for staff jobs. Also, programs typically focus on learning outcomes rather than financial results. Staff members often assess results by measuring reaction or learning. Consequently, a major barrier to ROI implementation is the need to orient the staff, change their attitudes, and teach them the necessary skills.

Faulty Needs Assessment

Many programs have been undertaken without an adequate needs assessment. Some of these programs were implemented for the wrong reasons, based on management requests or efforts to chase a popular fad or trend within the industry. If the program is not needed, its benefits will be minimal. An ROI calculation for an unnecessary program will likely yield a negative value. This likelihood deters practitioners from implementing ROI, because they fear facing such a negative reality.

Fear

Some departments and functions do not pursue evaluation of ROI because of fear of failure or fear of the unknown. Fear of failure can manifest in different ways. Designers, developers, facilitators, or program owners may be concerned about the consequence of a negative ROI. They may fear that ROI evaluations will be used as performance evaluation tools instead of process improvement tools. Use of the ROI Methodology may be feared due to a dislike of change. This fear of change, often based on unrealistic assumptions and a lack of knowledge, is a real barrier for many ROI implementations.

Lack of Discipline or Planning

Successfully implementing the ROI Methodology requires planning and a disciplined approach in order to keep the process on track. Implementation schedules, evaluation targets, ROI analysis plans, measurement and evaluation policies, and follow-up schedules are required. Staff members may not have enough discipline and determination to stay on course. This lack of staying power can become a barrier, particularly if measuring the ROI is not an immediate requirement. If the current senior management group does not require an ROI evaluation, the staff may not allocate time for the necessary planning and coordination. Only a carefully planned implementation will be successful.

False Assumptions

Many staff members have false assumptions about the ROI process that keep them from attempting ROI implementation. Some typical assumptions are the following:

- The impact of a program cannot be accurately calculated.

- Managers do not want to see the results of projects and programs expressed in monetary values.

- If the CEO does not ask for the ROI, he or she does not expect it.

- "I have a professional, competent staff; therefore, I do not have to justify the effectiveness of our programs."

- "Our programs are complex but necessary; therefore, they should not be subjected to an accountability process."

These false assumptions can become real barriers that impede the progress of ROI implementation.

Benefits of Using ROI

This section outlines several important benefits that can be derived from the implementation of the ROI Methodology within an organization.

Measurement of a Program's Contribution

Measuring ROI is the most accurate, credible, and widely used process to show the impact of a program. The staff will know the specific contribution from a select number of programs. The ROI will determine whether the benefits of a program, expressed in monetary values, have outweighed the costs. It will determine whether the program made a positive contribution to the organization and whether it was a good investment.

Clear Priorities

Calculating ROI in different areas will determine which programs contribute the most to an organization, allowing priorities to be established for high-impact programs. Successful programs can then be expanded into other areas (if those areas have similar needs) ahead of other programs. Inefficient programs can be redesigned and redeployed. Ineffective programs can be discontinued.

Focus on Results

The ROI Methodology is a results-based process that requires instructional designers, facilitators, participants, and support groups to concentrate on measurable objectives. This process tends to bring a focus on results to all programs, even those not targeted for an ROI evaluation. Thus, ROI implementation has the added benefit of improving the effectiveness of all programs.

Respect from Senior Executives and Program Sponsors

Measuring the ROI of programs is one of the best ways to earn the respect of your senior management team and your program sponsor. Senior executives always want to see ROI figures. They will appreciate efforts to connect programs with business impact and to show programs' monetary value. The sponsors who support, approve, or initiate programs will view ROI measurement as a breath of fresh air. They will be able to see an actual value for a program, building confidence in the decision to use the ROI process.

Positive Changes in Management Perceptions

The ROI Methodology, when applied consistently and comprehensively, can convince top management that projects and programs are investments, not expenses. Managers will see that programs make viable contributions to their objectives, thus increasing their respect for the function or department that produces those programs. Changing perceptions is an important step in building a partnership with management and increasing management support.

ROI Best Practices

Continuing progress with ROI implementation has provided an opportunity to determine specific strategies that are common among organizations pursuing the ROI Methodology. Several common strategies that are considered the best practices in measurement and evaluation have emerged. Although the following strategies are presented as a comprehensive framework, few organizations have adopted them all. However, parts of the strategy are practiced in each of the several hundred organizations involved in ROI certi-fication, which is described in the sixth book of the ROI Six Pack, *Communication and Implementation*.

Evaluation Targets

Evaluations targets were discussed in Chapter One. The targets for evaluation at each level are

Level 0, Inputs and Indicators	100 percent
Level 1, Reaction and Planned Action	100 percent
Level 2, Learning and Confidence	80–90 percent
Level 3, Application and Implementation	15–30 percent
Level 4, Impact and Consequences	10 percent
Level 5, ROI	5 percent

Establishing evaluation targets has two major advantages. First, the process provides benchmarks that the staff can use to clearly measure the accountability of all programs or any segment of a function. Second, adopting targets focuses more attention on the accountability process, communicating a strong message about the extent of commitment to measurement and evaluation.

Microlevel Evaluation

Evaluating an entire functional area—such as human resources, management development, technology, or quality—is difficult. The ROI Methodology is more effective when applied to one program that can be linked to a direct payoff. For this reason, ROI evaluation should be considered a microlevel activity that usually focuses on a single program or a few tightly integrated programs. The decision whether to evaluate several programs or just one program should involve consideration of the objectives of the programs, the timing of the programs, and the cohesiveness of the programs. Attempting to evaluate a group of programs conducted over a long period can be difficult, partly because the cause-and-effect relationship becomes more confusing and complex.

A Variety of Data Collection Methods

Best-practice companies use a variety of approaches to collect evaluation data. They avoid becoming aligned with one or two methods for data collection, recognizing that each program, setting, and situation is different and that, consequently, different techniques are needed to collect the data. Interviews, focus groups, and questionnaires work well in some situations. In others, action plans, performance contracts, and performance monitoring are needed to determine the specific impact of the program. Best-practice organizations deliberately match the data collection method with the program, following a set of criteria developed internally.

Isolation of the Program

One of the most critical elements of the ROI Methodology is attempting to isolate the impact of the program from other influences that may have occurred during the same period. Best-practice organizations recognize that many influences affect business impact measures. Although programs are implemented in harmony with other systems and processes, it is often necessary to determine the contribution of a single program, particularly when the owners or sponsors of separate programs or processes are different parties. Consequently, after a program is conducted, it usually can take only part of the credit for improved performance. When an ROI evaluation is planned, best-practice organizations attempt to use one or more methods to isolate the effects of the program. They go beyond the typical use of a control group arrangement, which has set the standard for this process for many years, exploring a variety of other techniques in order to arrive at a realistic estimate of the program's impact on output measures.

Sampling for ROI Calculations

Because of the resources required for the process, most programs cannot include ROI calculations. Therefore, organizations must determine how many ROI evaluations are appropriate. There is no prescribed formula, and the number of ROI evaluations depends on many variables, including

- Staff expertise in evaluation

- The nature and type of programs

- Resources that can be allocated to the process

- The level of management support for the department

- The organization's commitment to measurement and evaluation

- Pressure from others to show ROI calculations

Other variables specific to an organization may affect how many evaluations are performed. It is rare for organizations to use statistical sampling to select programs for ROI evaluation. For most, a statistical sampling approach requires far too many calculations and too much analysis. Using a practical approach, most organizations settle on evaluating one or two sessions of each of their most significant programs.

While statistically sound sampling is important, it is more important to consider the trade-off between resources available and the level of activity that management needs in order to feel confident in the ROI calculations. The primary objective of an ROI evaluation is not only to convince the staff that the process being evaluated works but also to show others (usually senior management) that the function or department being evaluated makes a difference. Therefore, the sampling plan must be developed with the input and approval of senior management. In the final analysis, the selection process should yield a level of sampling that allows senior management to feel comfortable in its assessment of the function or unit.

Conversion of Program Results to Monetary Values

Because ROI is needed for some programs, business impact data must be converted to monetary values. Best-practice organizations are not content to show that a program improved productivity, enhanced quality, reduced employee turnover, decreased absenteeism, or increased customer satisfaction. Going further, the organizations convert such data items to monetary units so that the benefits can be compared with the costs, leading, in turn, to an ROI calculation. Best-practice organizations take an extra step to develop a realistic value for their data items. For hard data items such as productivity, quality, or time, the conversion is relatively easy. However, for soft data items such as customer satisfaction, employee turnover, employee absenteeism, or job satisfaction, the conversion process is more difficult. Still, techniques are available and are used to make these conversions reasonably accurate.

Final Thoughts

Most professionals agree that more attention to measuring ROI is needed, and its use is expanding. The payoff for using ROI can be huge, and the ROI Methodology is not very difficult. The approaches, strategies, and techniques are not overly complex and can be used in a variety of settings. The combined and persistent efforts of practitioners and researchers will continue to refine the techniques and create successful applications.

Reference

Sibbet, D. "75 Years of Management Ideas and Practice, 1922–1997." *Harvard Business Review*, 1997, Supplement.

3

Who Should Use the ROI Methodology?

The ROI Methodology is not intended for just one type of organization. Bringing accountability to programs or processes is a concern for all organizations, regardless of their product, service, mission, or scope. Organizations have accountability issues, whether economic conditions are favorable or unfavorable. During positive economic times, expenditures increase, and organizational leaders have concerns about whether those investments are being properly allocated. During tough economic times, programs and projects that produce the best results are more likely to survive reorganization and restructuring efforts. A comprehensive evaluation system helps pinpoint the areas that will receive available funding.

The ROI Methodology grew quickly in private sector organizations. The growth has been slower in public sector organizations due to their culture and their reliance on cost-benefit analysis. For decades, the public sector has used cost-benefit analysis to support resource allocation. While cost-benefit analysis uses measures similar to those used for ROI calculation, it falls short of the balanced approach of a complete ROI evaluation. Today, therefore, public sector organizations are also moving toward use of the ROI Methodology so that all measures that explain the impact of a program can be taken into consideration.

The Typical Organization

The ROI Methodology is suitable for any organization, but some organizations that are currently implementing ROI as part of their evaluation process share similar characteristics. Typical character-istics include the following:

- *Large size*. Typically, organizations that implement the ROI Methodology are large. Whether in the public or private sector, large organizations have many different programs that are delivered to a diverse target audience, usually over a vast geographical area. Large organiza-tions also have the budget to develop comprehensive evaluation processes. Nonetheless, measurement of ROI should be built into the accountability process in smaller organizations as well. Small organizations have an even greater reason to conserve resources and ensure that they are getting the most out of their dollars. Using several cost-saving approaches described in book four, *Data Conversion*, small organizations (and larger organizations with limited budgets) can implement the ROI Methodology and achieve credible results.

- *Large, highly visible budget*. Whether the function is human resources, learning and development, quality, technology, or marketing, budgets have a way of escalating. The budgets for those functions almost always grow at a faster rate than the producer price index, which means that these processes are becom-ing much more expensive. Regardless of how it is benchmarked—whether as a total dollar amount, expenditure per employee, percentage of operating costs, or percentage of revenue—a large budget brings the need for additional measurement and evaluation.

Executives demand increased accountability for large expenditures.

- *Focus on measurement.* Organizations that implement the ROI Methodology focus on establishing a variety of measures throughout the organization. Organizations that use the Balanced Scorecard or other approaches at the strategic level are ideal candidates for the ROI Methodology because they already have a measurement-focused environment.

- *Key drivers requiring additional accountability.* In organizations that implement ROI measurement, one or more key drivers are in place, resulting in an increased focus on accountability. These issues and trends, presented in Chapter Two, drive the need to change current practices. In most situations, multiple drivers create interest in ROI accountability.

- *High level of change.* Organizations that use the ROI Methodology are usually undergoing significant change. As they adjust to competitive pressures, they are transforming, restructuring, and reorganizing. Such change often increases interest in bottom-line issues, resulting in a need for greater accountability.

The Typical Program

The ROI Methodology is used in all types of programs, ranging from technical training to child care for the disadvantaged. Exhibit 3.1 provides a sample of the various programs in which ROI has been used. The methodology can be applied to these types of programs and many more.

Exhibit 3.1. Typical Programs That Use the ROI Methodology

- Absenteeism control or reduction
- Business coaching
- Career development, career management
- Communications
- Compensation plans
- Compliance
- Diversity
- E-learning
- Employee benefits plans
- Employee relations
- Gainsharing plans
- Labor-management cooperation
- Leadership development
- Marketing and advertising
- Meeting planning
- Orientation, on-boarding
- Personal productivity and time management
- Procurement
- Project management
- Public policy
- Public relations
- Recruiting source (new)
- Retention management
- Safety incentive plans
- Selection tool (new)
- Self-directed teams
- Sexual harassment prevention
- Six Sigma
- Skill-based pay
- Strategy, policy
- Stress management
- Technical training
- Technology implementation
- Wellness, fitness

Although the ROI Methodology is being applied to a wide variety of programs, specific characteristics define the type of programs that should be considered. These characteristics include

- *Needs assessment*. Most programs evaluated by means of the ROI Methodology are the result of a comprehensive needs assessment that identified the program as an appropriate solution to a problem or an opportunity.

- *Major investment*. Programs to which the ROI Methodology is applied are usually expensive, representing a major investment of resources.

- *Long life cycle*. The programs are usually offered multiple times, rather than being one-time offerings.

- *Broad reach*. Programs evaluated with the ROI Methodology reach a large target audience, affecting more than just a single functional unit or work team.

- *High profile*. Programs have a great deal of visibility within their organization, raising interest, curiosity, and in some cases, skepticism.

- *Executive interest*. Often, a program that uses the ROI Methodology has piqued the interest of senior management, driving their interest in quantifying the economic contribution of the program.

Signs That an Organization Is Ready for the ROI Methodology

An organization that is ready to implement the ROI Methodology in its programs displays several revealing characteristics. Many of the signs in the following list reflect the key drivers discussed in

Chapter Two, which can cause pressure to pursue ROI measurement.

- *Pressure from senior management to measure results.*
  Such pressure can range from a direct requirement
  that program effectiveness be measured to a very
  subtle expression of concern about the accountability
  of a functional unit, department, or program.

- *Extremely low investment in measurement and evaluation.*
  Most organizations spend about 1 percent of their direct
  budget on measurement and evaluation processes.
  Investment significantly lower than this amount may
  indicate that little or no measurement and evaluation is
  taking place, suggesting a need for greater accountability. Expenditures in the 3 to 5 percent range indicate
  that programs and functions are already undergoing
  serious evaluation.

- *Recent disastrous results from programs.* Every organization has had one or more situations in which a major
  program was implemented with no success. When
  multiple occurrences of a program fail, the originating
  function or department often bears the blame. Such
  failures may force the implementation of measurement
  and evaluation processes in order to quickly determine
  the impact of programs or, more appropriately, to
  forecast ROI prior to implementation.

- A *new director or leader of a function.* A new leader is
  often a catalyst for change and may initiate a review of
  previous programs. New leaders do not carry the stigma
  of ownership, nor do they have any attachment to old
  programs; therefore, they are often more objective than

the previous leaders. New leaders are often good for an organization, perhaps partly because they increase the need for accountability. They want to know which programs are effective and which are not and thus may demand that evaluation processes be put in place if they do not already exist.

- *Some managers want to create leading-edge programs and functions.* Some managers strive to build leading-edge processes and functions. In order to do so, they build comprehensive measurement and evaluation processes into the strategy. These managers often set the pace for measurement and evaluation, highlighting the fact that they are serious about bringing accountability to their functions. These functions' measurement and evaluation systems have formal guidelines, and evaluation is built into the program development function from the beginning. Measurement and evaluation often begin with a thorough needs assessment to determine the best solution, then they monitor the progress of the program and determine the business impact.

- *Lack of management support for a department's efforts.* In some cases, the image of a department or function is so poor that management does not support its efforts. While the unsatisfactory image may be caused by a number of factors, increasing accountability within the department or function and focusing on improving systems and processes may shore up the unit's image.

Exhibit 3.2 provides a self-assessment to help an organization determine whether it is ready to implement the ROI Methodology.

Exhibit 3.2. Self-Check: Is Your Organization a Candidate for Implementation of the ROI Methodology?

Read each question and check the box that corresponds to the most appropriate level of agreement:

1 = Disagree; 5 = Agree

	DISAGREE 1	2	3	4	AGREE 5
1. My organization is considered a large organization with a variety of projects and programs.					
2. My function has a large budget that attracts the interest of senior management.					
3. My organization has a culture of measurement and is focused on establishing a variety of measures for all functions.					
4. My organization is undergoing significant change.					
5. There is pressure from senior management to measure the results of our programs.					
6. My function has a low investment in measurement and evaluation.					
7. My organization has experienced more than one program disaster in the past.					
8. My function has a new leader.					
9. My team would like to be the leader in evaluating programs and processes.					
10. The image of my function is less than satisfactory.					

	DISAGREE 1	2	3	4	AGREE 5
11. My clients are demanding that programs and processes show bottom-line results.					
12. My function competes with other functions in our organization for resources.					
13. Increased focus has been placed on linking programs and processes to the strategic direction of the organization.					
14. My function is a key player in change initiatives currently taking place in our organization.					
15. Our function's overall budget is growing, and we are required to prove the bottom-line value of our processes.					

Scoring

If you scored:

15–30	Your organization is not yet a candidate for the ROI Methodology.
31–45	Your organization is not a strong candidate for the ROI Methodology. However, you should start pursuing some type of measurement process.
46–60	Your organization is a candidate for building skills to implement the ROI Methodology. At this point there is no real pressure to show ROI, which means that you have the perfect opportunity to put the ROI Methodology in place within your organization and perfect the process before it becomes a requirement.
61–75	Your organization should already be implementing a comprehensive measurement and evaluation process, including ROI calculations.

Taking a Reactive Versus a Proactive Approach

Probably one of the most telling issues in regard to who experiences success using the ROI Methodology and who does not is the rationale for pursuing it. Collectively, we've had the pleasure of working with thousands of people who have made the decision to implement the ROI Methodology. We've watched some succeed at their efforts and some fail. One of the most important determinants of success or failure is taking a proactive approach instead of a reactive approach.

Reactive Approach

If individuals pursue measurement of ROI in reaction to a pressure point, a request, or an urgent need, implementation may be difficult. If an individual is attempting to justify a budget or an expenditure, gain support for a program, or defend a particular standpoint, that individual is pursuing ROI measurement from a difficult position, often in reaction to a request. Unfortunately, a request often comes with a short time frame and tremendous pressure to show a positive value. When this is the case, there is often not enough time to properly collect program data, which may be inadequate in both quality and quantity. Also, since there has been no opportunity to appropriately plan the program from the beginning, the results may be diminished, perhaps even negative. This is not the desired scenario. When this occurs, the chance of a failed ROI measurement process greatly increases.

Proactive Approach

The ideal scenario is proactive implementation of the ROI Methodology. In this situation, the interested individuals see the value of measuring ROI. They understand that they may need to show the value of their budget to executives in the future, but they are under no immediate pressure to do so. Or if there is pressure, it is in the form of encouragement or support, not an ultimate requirement. These individuals see that they must show the value of their budget just as other departments or functions often do. They know that to be a business partner and an ally in making their organization effective, they must be accountable for their resources and take steps to demonstrate the contribution of their department or function to the overall success of the organization. They realize that process improvement is essential and that ROI measurement is a process improvement method. It can make things better—make the program work when it is not working or make it work better when it is. Proactive individuals also use the ROI Methodology to change the entire image of their department or function so that it will be involved in important decisions and ultimately earn a seat at the table. This proactive approach forms the rationale for pursuing the ROI Methodology. When a proactive approach is used, success is almost guaranteed.

Final Thoughts

This chapter discussed who is best suited to use the ROI Methodology and to which programs ROI is best applied. In reality, any organization can evaluate any program using this process. However, the organization must be ready and willing to take on the task of measuring ROI. The individuals involved in the process must have the right mindset; they should be taking a proactive approach to measuring ROI and not reacting to a request or demand for data and results. This process takes time and money and should be reserved for programs that are perceived as large investments—ones that are being considered for expansion, elimination, or improvement. Most of all, programs from which value is needed but whose value is unknown are candidates for the ROI Methodology.

4

How to Build a Credible Process

Developing a credible and comprehensive measurement and evaluation process is much like putting together the pieces of a puzzle. Figure 4.1 shows the major elements of this evaluation puzzle.

The first piece of the puzzle is the evaluation framework. This framework defines the levels at which programs are evaluated and how data are captured at different times and from different sources. Basically, these levels represent the categories of data collected and analyzed for the various stakeholders in the program.

The second piece of the puzzle is the process model for the ROI Methodology. The process model is critical because it depicts systematic steps that ensure consistent application of the evaluation methodology. The model shows step by step how and when to collect and analyze the data categorized by the five levels.

The third piece of the evaluation puzzle is operating standards and philosophy. These standards build credibility into the process by supporting a systematic methodology and a conservative approach to ROI evaluation. The standards, presented as the Twelve Guiding Principles in this book, also support consistency in the evaluation process.

Case studies showing real-world applications of the process are the fourth piece of the puzzle. Case studies describe the practical applications of the process as well as the use of the standards. It

Figure 4.1. The Evaluation Puzzle

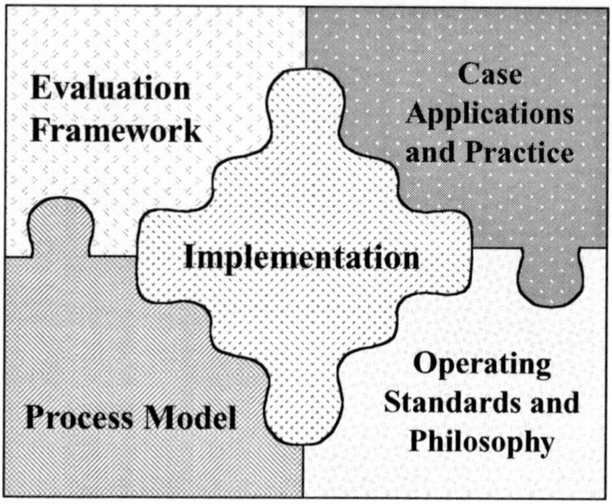

Source: Phillips, 2001.

is real-life applications that move the first three puzzle pieces from theory to practice. Case studies provide the initial step for the fifth piece of the evaluation puzzle.

The final piece of the puzzle, implementation, brings together the other four pieces to implement the ROI Methodology. Critical elements of implementation, which will be discussed later in this chapter, ensure that the evaluation process is fully integrated into the organization; that the organization develops the skills, procedures, and guidelines necessary for success; and that a comprehensive communication strategy is in place to ensure that the process is used to its fullest extent and that credibility with key stakeholders is maintained.

Together, the five pieces of the evaluation puzzle form a comprehensive measurement and evaluation system that contains a balanced set of measures, has credibility, and can be replicated from one group to another.

The Evaluation Framework

The evaluation framework, described briefly in Chapter One, is the first piece of the evaluation puzzle.

The concept of levels of evaluation evolved from work by Donald Kirkpatrick, which he began publishing in 1959 (Kirkpatrick, 1959). At that time, Kirkpatrick suggested four specific steps of program evaluation:

1. Reaction
2. Learning
3. Job behavior
4. Results

During the next three decades, although the concept of steps morphed into the concept of levels, no effort was made to refine the fundamental premise or develop a system of standards to support the collection and analysis of data that would be gathered through the steps. It was in the 1970s and 1980s that others began to make some improvements on the concept of evaluation levels. Table 4.1 shows the five-level framework introduced in the 1980s by Jack Phillips (1983). The levels shown represent important adjustments and refinements of Kirkpatrick's initial steps.

Kirkpatrick's work provided the initial steps for evaluation of training programs. However, the need to take evaluation further has intensified in the past two decades. Executives are increasingly requiring the training and performance improvement function to demonstrate the value it brings to an organization. Other support functions need a process through which to demonstrate value too. The most common measure of value-added benefits is return on investment (Horngren, 1982; Anthony and Reece, 1983). ROI is the ratio of earnings (net benefits) to investment (costs) (Kearsley, 1982).

Table 4.1. Phillips's Five Levels of Evaluation

Level	Description	Focus	Frequency of Use	Comments	Challenges
1. Reaction and Planned Action	Measures participants' reaction to the program, stakeholders' satisfaction with the program, and the actions planned as a result of the program, if feasible	Consumer	Very high	Data at this level are very easy to measure. Level 1 data are usually measured in 100% of evaluations but have very little value from the client's perspective.	Data collection is frequently automated, and data must be used appropriately.
2. Learning	Measures skills, knowledge, or attitude changes resulting from the program	Consumer	High	Data are more difficult to measure than in Level 1. This level of evaluation is very important in learning and development functions but less important in other functions.	Data collection is sometimes automated and data must be used appropriately.

Level	Description	Focus	Frequency of Use	Comments	Challenges
3. Application and Imple-mentation	Measures changes in behavior on the job and specific application and implementation of the program	Consumer and client	Moderate	Data collected at this level are critical for most programs in assessing whether any behavior or process change related to the program has occurred.	An organization or unit must work hard to get good data and keep costs and disruption low.
4. Business Impact	Captures changes in business impact related to the program	Client	Occasional	Data are easy to measure but are perceived as difficult to analyze.	Isolating the effects of the program on the data is difficult but necessary to determine a valid relationship between the program and reported results.
5. Return on Investment	Compares the monetary values of the impact with the costs of the program	Client	Rare	Data at this level are more difficult to analyze but constitute the most valuable data set available.	This analysis is pursued for only a limited number of projects.

Table 4.1 not only reemphasizes the definitions of each level provided in Chapter One but shows some of the characteristics of the different levels. The focus moves from the consumer at the lower levels to the client at the higher levels. In other words, key clients who pay for projects and programs are more interested in the higher levels of evaluation, particularly Levels 4 and 5. The consumers involved in the programs and projects may have more interest in their own reaction and what they are learning from the program than in the higher levels of data. Ironically, the frequency of data collection is higher at the lower levels than it is at the higher levels, partly because collecting data at the lower levels is easier, even though Level 4 data are not difficult to capture in most organizations. The daunting problem, however, is connecting Level 4 measures to the program. The challenges of data collection and analysis increase as measurement is pursued at the higher levels. Nonetheless, the measurement landscape has essentially changed so that it now includes a requirement for higher levels of data, up to and including ROI.

Whereas Kirkpatrick's fourth step stops with identifying the results of the program (Level 4, Results), the ROI Methodology refines Level 4 and then creates a fifth level. First, at Level 4, the results of the program need to be isolated. Ignoring the other factors that could have contributed to the improvement in Level 4 measures would be inappropriate; isolation must occur in order to answer the question, "How does the organization know that the program caused the reported results?"

Next, to move from Level 4 to Level 5, the steps of cost-benefit analysis are employed. Level 4 measures (the ones that have been connected to the program through isolation) are converted to monetary values and then compared with the fully loaded cost of the program. The steps for moving from Level 4 to Level 5 are not new (cost-benefit analysis has been around for centuries); however, the economic indicator resulting from cost-benefit analysis alone

Table 4.2. Phillips's Five-Level Evaluation Framework Compared with Cost-Benefit Analysis

	Phillips's Five-Level Framework (ROI Methodology)	Cost-benefit analysis
Measures participant reaction to program	✓	
Measures learning resulting from program	✓	
Measures applications and behavior resulting from program	✓	
Measures impact and benefits of program	✓	✓
Measures ROI	✓	✓
Isolates effects of program	✓	
Determines cost of program	✓	✓
Converts program benefits to monetary values	✓	✓
Identifies intangible benefits of program	✓	✓

provides an insufficient story of program success. By using the first four levels of program evaluation, adding the step to isolate the impact of the program, and bringing in benefit-cost analysis, the ROI Methodology tells a complete story of program success. In addition, improvement data are developed that can enhance future program implementations. Table 4.2 provides a comparison of the Phillips framework and the cost-benefit analysis.

Although the distinction between the Phillips framework and cost-benefit analysis is important, not all programs are evaluated at all five levels. Perhaps the best explanation for this is that as the level of evaluation increases, so does its difficulty and expense.

A comprehensive ROI evaluation takes time and resources, so conducting one for every program is not feasible. Only a limited number of programs should be targeted for evaluation at the ROI level, as discussed in Chapter Two.

It is important to note that when programs are evaluated at a higher level, they must be evaluated at the lower levels as well. A chain of impact should occur as participants react and plan action (Level 1) based on the skills and knowledge acquired during the program (Level 2) that will be applied on the job (Level 3) to produce business impact (Level 4). If success is achieved with business impact and the cost of the program was appropriate, a positive ROI (Level 5) will occur. If measurements are not taken at each of these levels, it is difficult to conclude that the results achieved are a result of the program and to understand how the results, including ROI, evolved.

The Process Model

The second piece of the evaluation puzzle is the process model for the ROI Methodology, which was briefly explored in Chapter One. The process model shows a systematic, step-by-step process that will ensure that the methodology is implemented consistently. The process model consists of four stages: evaluation planning, data collection, data analysis, and reporting of results.

The Operating Standards: Guiding Principles

Operating standards, the third piece of the evaluation puzzle, help ensure that the evaluation process is consistent and that a conservative approach is taken. Standards and guiding principles keep the evaluation credible and allow the process to be replicated. Twelve Guiding Principles are used as operating standards in implementing the ROI Methodology (Phillips, 1997).

1. Report the Complete Story

When conducting a higher-level evaluation, collect data at lower levels. ROI is a critical measure, but it is only one of six measures necessary to explain the full impact of the program. Therefore, lower levels of data must be included in the analysis. Data at the lower levels also provide important information that may be helpful in making adjustments for future program implementation.

2. Conserve Important Resources

When planning a higher-level evaluation, the previous level of evaluation is not required to be comprehensive. Lower-level measures are critical in telling the complete story, and they cannot be omitted. However, shortcuts can be taken in order to conserve resources. For example, when the client is interested in business impact, shortcuts can be taken at Levels 1, 2, and 3.

3. Enhance Credibility

When collecting and analyzing data, use only the most credible sources. Credibility is the most important factor in the measurement and evaluation process. Without it, the results are meaningless. Using the most credible source, which is often the participants, will enhance the perception that the data analysis and results are accurate and of high quality.

4. Be Conservative

When analyzing data, select the most conservative alternative for calculations. This principle is at the heart of the evaluation process. A conservative approach lowers the ROI and helps build the needed credibility with the target audience. Being conservative is better than providing a generous estimate and having results that are not believable.

5. Account for Other Factors

Use at least one method to isolate the effects of a program. This step is imperative. Without some method of isolating the effects of the program, the evaluation results will be considered inaccurate and overstated.

6. Account for Missing Data

If no improvement data are available for a population or from a specific source, assume that little or no improvement has occurred. If participants do not provide data—for example, if they are no longer part of the organization or they now perform a different function—it should be assumed that little or no improvement has occurred. To assume otherwise would damage the credibility of the evaluation. This ultraconservative approach will further enhance the credibility of the results.

7. Adjust Estimates for Error

Adjust estimates of improvement for potential errors of estimation. This principle contributes to a conservative approach. Using estimates is a common process in reporting financial and benefit-cost information. To enhance the credibility of estimated data used in ROI evaluation, estimates are weighted with a level of confidence in the estimate by the respondent, adjusting the estimate for potential error.

8. Omit the Extremes

Avoid using extreme data items and unsupported claims when calculating ROI. Again, to maintain the credibility of results, steps should be taken to be conservative in the analysis. Extreme data items can skew results toward the low side or the high side. To eliminate the influence of extreme data items, they should be omitted from the analysis. Also, when benefits are presented with no explanation of how they were derived, they should be omitted from the analysis.

9. Capture Annual Benefits for Short-Term Programs

Use only the first year of annual benefits in ROI analysis of short-term solutions. For most programs, if benefits are not quickly realized, the program is probably not worth the cost. Therefore, for short-term programs, only first-year benefits should be considered. For longer-term programs in which implementation spans a year or more, multiple-year benefits can be captured.

10. Account for All Program Costs

Fully load all costs of a solution, project, or program when analyzing ROI. All costs of the program should be tabulated, beginning with the cost of the needs analysis and ending with the cost of the evaluation. In a conservative approach, the costs are loaded into the analysis, reducing the ROI.

11. Report Intangible Benefits

Intangible measures are defined as measures that are purposely not converted to monetary values. Understanding the significance of intangible measures and how to work with them properly is important. Specific rules must be developed for deciding when to leave data in the form of intangible benefits. If data can be credibly converted to monetary values with minimum resources, they should become tangible. Otherwise, they can be reported as intangible benefits.

12. Communicate Results

Communicate the results of the ROI Methodology to all key stakeholders. Many stakeholders may need to receive the data from an ROI evaluation. Four key groups will always need the information: the participants, the participants' immediate managers, the key sponsor or client, and the function's or department's staff.

Collectively, these twelve principles will ensure that a conservative approach is taken to ROI measurement, that the evaluation can be replicated, and that the ROI for programs and projects can be compared with the ROI of other operational processes and initiatives.

Case Applications and Practice

A critical piece of the evaluation puzzle is the development of case studies to show success, to promote programs, or to justify new programs. Case studies from other organizations can also be used for benchmarking or as examples of success. Today, almost three hundred case studies have been published about this methodology, and more are being published each year. Cases have been published about the use of the ROI Methodology in a variety of settings and also in different countries, cultures, and languages. Go to www.roiinstitute.net for more details on published case studies.

Case studies within specific industries may indicate the status of ROI measurement in organizations similar to your own—organizations that may be addressing issues and targeting concerns similar to those in your organization. Case studies from a global perspective provide evidence of progress in ROI measurement in a variety of organizations and industries. Case studies provide support to practitioners, managers, and executives who are interested in learning how to apply the ROI Methodology.

While the use of case studies from other organizations is helpful in understanding the merits of ROI measurement and the success of specific programs, studies within an organization are more powerful and persuasive for individuals in that organization, displaying evidence of success through use of the ROI Methodology in internal programs.

Implementation

The final piece of the evaluation puzzle is implementation. The best tool, technique, or model will not be successful unless it is properly used and becomes a routine part of operations. As with any change, the people affected by the implementation of a comprehensive measurement and evaluation process may resist it. Some of the resistance will be based on real barriers. Part of it, however, may be based on misunderstandings and perceived problems. In both cases, the organization must work to overcome the resistance by carefully and methodically implementing the ROI Methodology, using a few critical steps:

1. Assign responsibilities.
2. Develop skills.
3. Develop an implementation plan.
4. Prepare or revise evaluation guidelines.
5. Brief managers on the evaluation process.

Assign Responsibilities

To ensure successful implementation of the ROI Methodology, responsibilities are assigned up front—before implementation begins. Who will lead the evaluation effort? Will evaluation be integrated into the department or function, or will it report to the CFO? Is it more appropriate to contract with a third-party evaluation provider and have only an internal coordinator? These questions and others must be considered when implementing any evaluation strategy.

Develop Skills

Another key step in successful implementation is the development of skills and capabilities. Skills in evaluation planning, data collection design and analysis, and communication are important to successful implementation. A complete understanding of each step in the evaluation process simplifies implementation, reducing the stress and frustration often associated with jumping from one process to another.

Develop an Implementation Plan

Planning for implementation will save time and money. By using a basic set of criteria to review existing programs as well as proposed new programs, a department or function can develop an implementation plan. This plan will assist in determining which programs will be evaluated and at which levels (by using the criteria discussed in Chapters Two and Three) as well as how the necessary resources will be allocated.

Along with an implementation plan for selecting programs for different levels of evaluation, a project plan should be developed to help manage the overall evaluation process. From a practical standpoint, this project plan supports the transition from the present situation to a desired future situation. Exhibit 4.1 shows a sample project plan. This particular evaluation project includes skill development as well as implementation of ROI for several programs. The project plan is a summary of the evaluation. The ten key tasks in the following list should be addressed in each project plan. Other tasks should be considered for specific projects.

1. *Review of existing programs, processes, reports, and data.* This step is essential in order to understand past practices and how to incorporate the new methodology most effectively.

2. *Skill development.* Developing the skills necessary to implement the ROI Methodology is essential for its complete integration into the function or department.

3. *Finalization of evaluation planning documents.* Completing the planning documents that are necessary to implement the ROI Methodology is critical in order to ensure that every step of the process is taken and that key stakeholders are in agreement with those steps.

4. *Collection of data for evaluation.* This step represents the data collection process. This process includes selecting the appropriate instrument, identifying the most credible sources of data, and determining the most appropriate timing of data collection.

5. *Analysis of the data.* This step represents the time necessary to analyze the data after it is collected.

6. *Development of reports.* Developing a variety of reports helps address the needs of specific audiences. A complete impact study should be developed for the department's records. After the executive management group understands the evaluation process, it will be necessary to prepare a brief (in some cases only one page) summary to give executives key results without overwhelming them with details.

7. *Presentation of evaluation results.* Different audiences need different information. In the initial implementation of the ROI Methodology, the results should be presented in a formal setting to ensure clear communication about the process itself. Presentation of the results to the staff members may take place in a less formal setting, such as a weekly staff meeting.

8. *Development of scorecard framework.* In the Exhibit 4.1 example, the client requested a summary scorecard that would report the results for all the function's projects and programs.

9. *Development of guidelines.* As the ROI Methodology is implemented and integrated into a function, guidelines are developed to ensure consistent long-term implementation.

10. *Manager briefings.* Management understanding of the ROI evaluation process is critical. Managers who are not involved in a particular evaluation project might still be interested in the process. Manager briefings are a way to communicate not only the results of the evaluation but also about the process in general.

Exhibit 4.1. Project Plan

	OCT	NOV	DEC	JAN	FEB	MAR	APR	MAY	JUN	JUL	AUG	SEP
Review existing programs, processes, reports, and data	▓											
Develop skills		▓										
Finalize evaluation planning documents			▓	▓								
Collect data for evaluation				▓	▓	▓	▓	▓	▓			
Analyze data								▓	▓	▓	▓	
Develop reports									▓		▓	
Present evaluation results												▓
Develop scorecard framework									▓	▓	▓	
Develop guidelines						▓	▓	▓	▓	▓		
Brief managers									▓			

Each individual program evaluation will have individual project plans that detail the steps necessary to complete the project as well as keep the evaluation project on track. Planning is the key to successful implementation of the ROI Methodology.

Prepare or Revise Evaluation Guidelines

Guidelines keep the implementation process on track. A clear set of guidelines will help ensure that the process continues as designed when changes in staff or management occur. Guidelines also establish the evaluation process as an integral part of the overall strategy of a unit or department. Guidelines should be updated or revised as implementation progresses, incorporating what is learned during the process.

Brief Managers on the Evaluation Process

Communicating to managers about the evaluation process as it proceeds will help enlist their support during the implementation process. The unknown can often become a barrier, so if the organization makes the effort to explain each step, managers will generally be more likely to understand and support the evaluation efforts.

Final Thoughts

Implementing an evaluation method begins with planning. Setting up an evaluation framework that supports and sustains the process is critical. The ROI Methodology is a step-by-step process that collects six types of data, including ROI, through its five-level framework. When implemented properly, it is a credible and comprehensive measurement and evaluation system. It must also be supported by the Twelve Guiding Principles, which add credibility and consistency by ensuring a conservative process.

References

Anthony, R. N., and Reece, J. S. *Accounting Text and Cases.* New York: Irwin, 1983.

Horngren, C. T. *Cost Accounting.* Upper Saddle River, N. J.: Prentice Hall, 1982.

Kearsley, G. *Costs, Benefits, and Productivity in Training Systems.* Reading, Mass.: Addison-Wesley, 1982.

Kirkpatrick, D. L. "Techniques for Evaluating Programs." *Journal of the American Society of Training Directors*, Nov. 1959.

Phillips, J. J. *Handbook of Training and Evaluation Methods.* (1st ed.) Houston, Tex.: Gulf, 1983.

Phillips, J. J. *Return on Investment in Training and Performance Improvement Programs.* Boston: Butterworth-Heinemann, 1997.

Phillips, J. *The Consultant's Scorecard: Tracking Results and Bottom-Line Impact of Consulting Projects.* New York: McGraw-Hill, 2001.

5

Inhibitors of Implementation

Although progress is being made in the implementation of the ROI Methodology on many fronts, a variety of factors can inhibit implementation of the concept. Some factors are real barriers; others are perceptions based on myths. The key to overcoming barriers is distinguishing reality from myth and taking steps to overcome the barriers.

Barriers to Implementation

A variety of barriers can deter or prevent successful implementation of the ROI Methodology. While the barriers may be real, steps can be taken to overcome them.

Costs and Time

A comprehensive measurement and evaluation process that includes ROI will add additional costs and time to programs, although the added amount should not be excessive. The additional costs should be no more than 3 to 5 percent of the total budget. The additional investment in ROI should be offset by the results achieved from implementation (for example, elimination or prevention of unproductive or unprofitable programs). Barriers of cost and time stop many ROI implementations early in the process. However, there are a few shortcuts and cost-saving approaches that

Exhibit 5.1. Tips and Techniques for Reducing the Cost of Implementing the ROI Methodology

- Build evaluation into the process.
- Develop criteria for selecting program measurement levels.
- Plan for evaluation early.
- Share the responsibilities involved in evaluation.
- Require participants to conduct major steps, such as providing impact data or converting measures to monetary values.
- Use shortcut methods of performing major steps, such as using questionnaires.
- Use estimates.
- Develop internal capability in developing data collection instruments and analyzing data.
- Streamline the reporting process.
- Use technology.

Source: Phillips and Burkett, 2001.

can be taken to help reduce the cost of the actual implementation. Exhibit 5.1 presents ten ways to save time and money.

Lack of Skills

Many staff members do not understand ROI or do not have the basic skills necessary to apply the process. Also, many programs focus more on qualitative feedback data (Level 1) than quantitative results (Levels 4 and 5). Therefore, a possible barrier to implementation is the need for overall orientation and for a change in the attitude and skills of staff members. Suggestions for building ROI evaluation skills include

- Attending public workshops

- Becoming certified in the ROI Methodology

- Conducting internal workshops

- Starting with less comprehensive evaluations and building skills toward a more comprehensive evaluation

- Participating in evaluation networking forums

Faulty or Inadequate Initial Analysis

Many projects and programs do not include an adequate initial analysis and assessment of their evaluation process. Some functions implement programs for the wrong reasons, such as management requests or efforts to chase a popular fad or trend in the industry. If a program is not necessary or not based on business needs, it may not produce enough benefits to overcome the costs. An ROI calculation for an unnecessary program will likely yield a negative value. This is a real barrier for evaluating many programs, because many individuals do not want to acknowledge that their program is not working as expected. To overcome this barrier, develop or enhance the initial analysis process. Become engaged with the client to gain a deeper understanding of the needs from which a project arises. This helps to ensure that an appropriate program is implemented, yielding a greater ROI.

Fear

Some staff members do not pursue ROI because of a fear of failure or a fear of the unknown. Fear of failure appears in several forms. Some people are concerned about the consequences of a negative ROI. They perceive the evaluation process as an individual performance evaluation rather than a process improvement tool. For others, a comprehensive measurement process can stir up the traditional fear of change and the unknown. Although often based on unrealistic assumptions and a lack of knowledge about the process, the fear can be so strong that it becomes a real barrier to many ROI implementations. Ensuring that staff members understand the process and its intent is the key to removing this fear.

Discipline and Planning

A successful ROI implementation requires planning and a disciplined approach. Implementation schedules, transition plans, evaluation targets, ROI analysis plans, measurement and evaluation policies, and follow-up schedules are required. The practitioner may not have enough discipline and determination to stay the course. This lack of will can become a barrier, particularly when no immediate pressures to measure ROI exist. If clients or other executives are not demanding ROI, staff members may not allocate time for planning and coordination. Also, other pressures and priorities often take precedence over ROI implementation. Planning the work and working the plan are key to successful implementation.

ROI Myths

Although most practitioners recognize the ROI Methodology as an important addition to measurement and evaluation, they often struggle with how to address the issue. Many professionals see it as a ticket to increased funding and prosperity for their programs. They believe that without it they may be lost in the shuffle and that with it they may gain the respect they need to continue moving their department or function forward. Regardless of their motivation, the key questions are, "Is the ROI Methodology a feasible process that can be implemented with reasonable resources?" and, "Will implementation of ROI measurement provide the benefits necessary to make it a useful, routine tool?" The answers to these questions may lead to debate and even to controversy.

The controversy surrounding the ROI Methodology stems from misunderstandings about the process, what it can and cannot do, and how it should be implemented within an organization. These misunderstandings are summarized in this section as fifteen myths about the ROI Methodology. The myths have been revealed during years of experience with ROI and from perceptions observed during hundreds of projects and workshops. Along with each myth, we present an appropriate explanation.

ROI Is Too Complex for Most Users

This myth is a problem because of a few highly complex ROI models that have been publicly presented. Unfortunately, these models have done little to help users and have caused confusion about ROI. The ROI Methodology is a basic financial formula for accountability that is simple and understandable: earnings are divided by investment; earnings are the net benefits from the program, and the investment equals the actual cost of the program. Straying from this basic formula can add confusion and create misunderstanding. The ROI model provides a step-by-step, systematic process that allows users to collect and analyze data important to overall program improvement. These data also help users explain why the ROI is what it is and how to improve it in the future. Each step is taken separately, and issues are addressed for that particular step. The decisions are made incrementally throughout the process. This method helps make a complex process simpler and more manageable.

ROI Is Expensive, Consuming Too Many Critical Resources

The ROI Methodology can become expensive if it is not carefully organized, precisely controlled, and properly implemented. While the cost of an external ROI impact study can be significant, many actions can be taken to lower costs, as shown earlier in Exhibit 5.1.

If Senior Management Does Not Require ROI, There Is No Need to Pursue It

This myth affects the most innocent bystanders. It is easy to be lulled into providing evaluation and measurement that simply preserves the status quo, believing that no pressure or request means no requirement. The truth is that if senior executives have seen only

Level 1 reaction data, they may not ask for higher-level data because they think those data are not available. In some cases, leaders have convinced top management that programs cannot be evaluated at the ROI level or that the specific impact of a program cannot be determined. Given these conditions, it comes as no surprise that some top managers are not asking for Level 5 (ROI) data.

This kind of thinking may cause another problem later. Changes in corporate leadership sometimes initiate important paradigm shifts. New leaders often require proof of accountability. The process of implementing the ROI Methodology in an organization takes time—about twelve to eighteen months for many organizations; it is not a quick fix. When senior executives suddenly ask for data that show the value of a function or program, they may expect quick results. Because this type of short-term request can happen unexpectedly, departments or functions should initiate ROI evaluation long before they are asked for ROI data.

ROI Is a Passing Fad

Unfortunately, this perception applies to many processes being introduced in organizations today. However, the need to account for expenditures will always be present, and the ROI Methodology provides the ultimate level of accountability. ROI has a rich history of use as an accountability tool. In the past, ROI was used mostly to measure investment in equipment and new plants. Today, its use is being extended to many other areas. In the future, its flexibility and broad applicability will ensure that ROI continues to be used as a tool for measurement and evaluation.

ROI Is Only One Type of Data

This is a common misunderstanding. The ROI calculation represents one type of data that shows the benefits versus the costs for a program. However, when the complete five-level evaluation framework is used, six types of data are generated, representing both qualitative and quantitative data and often involving data from different sources, making the ROI Methodology a rich source for a variety of data.

ROI Is Not Future-Oriented; It Reflects Only Past Performance

Unfortunately, many evaluation processes are past-oriented and reflect only what has already happened in a program. This is the only way to have an accurate assessment of impact. However, the ROI Methodology can easily be adapted to forecast ROI for a program.

ROI Is Rarely Used by Organizations

This myth is easily dispelled when the evidence is fully examined. More than 3,000 organizations use the ROI Methodology, and at least one hundred case studies on its implementation have been published. Leading organizations throughout the world, including businesses of all sizes and from all sectors, use the ROI Methodology to increase accountability and improve programs. This process is also being used in the nonprofit, educational, and government sectors. There is no doubt that it is a widely used process that is growing in use.

The ROI Methodology Cannot Be Easily Replicated

This is an understandable concern. In theory, any process worthy of implementation is one that can be replicated from one study to another. For example, if two people conducted an ROI evaluation on the same program, would they obtain the same results? Fortunately, the ROI Methodology is a systematic process with specific standards and guiding principles, so the likelihood of two evaluators obtaining the same results is high. And because it is a process that involves step-by-step procedures, the ROI Methodology can be replicated from one program to another.

ROI Is Not a Credible Process; It Is Too Subjective

This myth has evolved because some ROI evaluations involving estimates have been promoted in the literature and at conferences. Many ROI studies have been conducted without the use of estimates. The issue of estimates often surfaces during attempts to isolate the effects of a program from other influences. Using estimates from the participants is only one of several techniques used to isolate the effects of a program. Other techniques involve analytical approaches such as the use of control groups and trend line analysis. Sometimes, estimating is used in other steps of the ROI process, such as converting data to monetary values or estimating output in the data collection phase. In each of these situations, other options are often available, but for reasons of convenience or economics, estimation is often used. While the use of estimates may be the least ideal situation when evaluating ROI, estimates can be extremely reliable when they are obtained carefully, adjusted for error, and reported appropriately. The accounting, engineering, and technology fields routinely require the use of estimates, often without question or concern.

ROI Is Not Credible When Evaluating Soft-Skill Programs

ROI is often most effective in soft-skill programs. Soft skills such as training and learning often influence hard data items such as output, quality, cost, or time. Case after case shows successful application of the ROI Methodology to programs in areas such as team building, leadership, communications, and empowerment. Additional examples of successful ROI implementation can be found in compliance programs in areas such as diversity, sexual harassment prevention, and policy implementation.

ROI Is Only for Manufacturing and Service Organizations

Although initial studies on ROI appeared in the manufacturing sector, the service sector quickly picked up the process as a useful tool.

After that, use of the ROI Methodology migrated to the nonprofit sector, and organizations such as hospitals and health care firms began endorsing and using the process. Next, ROI evaluation moved around the world through the government sector, and now, educational institutions are using the ROI Methodology. Several educational institutions use ROI to measure the impact of their formal degree programs and less-structured continuing education programs.

Isolation of the Influence of Factors Other Than the Program Is Not Always Possible

Isolating the effects of influences external to a program is always achievable when using the ROI Methodology. At least nine ways to isolate the influence of other factors are available, and at least one method will work in any given situation. The challenge is selecting the appropriate isolation method for the resources and accuracy needed in each situation. This myth probably stems from unsuccessful attempts at using a control group arrangement—a classic way of isolating the effect of a program. In practice, a control group does not work in a majority of situations, causing some researchers to abandon the issue of isolating other factors. In reality, many other techniques provide accurate, reliable, and valid methods for isolating the effects of a program.

Measurement of On-the-Job Activities Is Impossible Because Post-Program Control of Application Is Impossible

This myth is fading as organizations face the reality that knowledge transfer is critical if change is to occur as a result of a program or process, and as leaders within organizations realize the importance of measuring on-the-job results. Although the program staff does not have direct control over what happens in the workplace, it does have influence on the learning transfer process. A program must be considered within the context of the workplace; the program is owned by the organization. Many individuals and groups may be involved with objectives that push expectations beyond the classroom or keyboard. Objectives focus on application and impact data used in the ROI analysis. Also, the partnership that is often needed between key managers produces objectives that drive the program. In effect, a process with partnerships and a common framework to drive the results—not just classroom activity—is necessary to ensure that application of new knowledge is transferred to improved job performance.

ROI Is Appropriate Only for Large Organizations

While large organizations with enormous budgets have the most interest in ROI, smaller organizations can also use the process, particularly when it is simplified and built into their programs. Organizations with as few as fifty employees have successfully applied the ROI Methodology, using it as a tool for increasing accountability and involvement in their programs.

The ROI Methodology Has No Standards

An important problem facing measurement and evaluation is a lack of standardization or consistency. Questions that are often asked include, "What is a good ROI?" "What should be included in the costs so that I can compare my data with other data?" and, "When should specific data be included in the ROI value instead of left as an intangible benefit?" While these questions are not easily answered, some help can be found in this book. The ROI Methodology has Twelve Guiding Principles, which are discussed in Chapter Four. These principles give consistency and rigor to the ROI measurement process. In addition, some of the more specific questions posed in this section will be answered in subsequent books in this series.

It's All About Change Management

The material in this chapter illustrates that implementing the ROI Methodology is about more than simply putting a measurement system in place. Effective use of the process requires a change in the way organizations implement programs and projects. Evaluation data must be acted upon; in knowledge roles, transfer must be recognized and put into action. Previous processes must be unlearned and new knowledge acquired and ultimately applied. It is about change management.

Any book about the steps of change management would apply to this process. Implementing the ROI Methodology brings change to the following individuals:

- Clients, who request or initiate projects or programs

- Program designers and analysts, who link projects to business results

- Program designers and developers, who build or create projects or programs to focus on results

- Participants and other stakeholders actively involved in the process, who must change their perception of their role in program success (specifically, what they have to do to ensure that success)

- Senior executives, who provide the funding for projects or programs and who expect results

- Organizers, project managers, and facilitators, who administer and teach programs

- Evaluators, who must change the way they evaluate programs

Because so much change is involved, much effort is required to ensure that it is properly implemented. The sixth book in this series, *Communication and Implementation*, will focus on some of the issues involved in implementing this method.

Exhibit 5.2. Checklist for ROI Implementation

- Assess progress with evaluation and readiness for ROI implementation.
- Organize a task force or network to initiate the process.
- Develop and publish a philosophy or mission statement concerning accountability and ROI of all programs.
- Clarify roles and responsibilities of task force members.
- Develop a transition plan, detailing the steps necessary to successfully implement ROI.
- Set targets for evaluating programs at the various levels of evaluation.
- Develop guidelines to ensure that ROI is implemented completely and consistently.
- Build staff skills in using the ROI Methodology.
- Establish a management support system or champions of ROI.
- Through communication, enhance management support, commitment, and participation in the implementation of ROI.
- Achieve short-term results by evaluating one program at a time.
- Communicate results to stakeholders.
- Teach the process to others in order to enhance their understanding of ROI.
- Establish a quality review process to ensure that the evaluation process remains consistent and credible.

Next Steps

Now that the ROI Methodology has been explained, assess your knowledge by taking the ROI Quiz at the end of this chapter. Then, to help you get started with ROI implementation, Exhibit 5.2 provides a checklist of steps. As you make progress and issues surface, numerous resources will be available to assist in implementing ROI. The Appendix at the end of this book lists some of these resources.

Final Thoughts

So what is the bottom line on ROI? ROI has been used for generations to show the value of programs, projects, and processes within organizations. The ROI calculation is the financial ratio used by accountants, chief financial officers, and executives to measure the return on all investments. The term *ROI* is familiar to all executives and operational managers. It is not a fly-by-night new catchphrase with an unknown meaning that can only be explained through elaborate presentations and is only understood in a very small area of the organization.

The ROI Methodology described in this book goes beyond a benefit-cost comparison. Rather, it provides a balanced viewpoint of projects and programs by taking into consideration participant reactions, learning, application of new skills and knowledge, and business impact achieved as a result of the program. The process presents a complete picture of program success. Further, by including the critical step of isolating the effects of the program, the impact on business can be further linked to programs. The process presented in this book is based on sound research and conservative guidelines. Although not all programs should be evaluated at the ROI level, for those meeting specific criteria, ROI is a credible approach to providing evidence of a program's financial impact on the organization. A thorough and complete understanding of the ROI Methodology can help eliminate fears and overcome barriers to its implementation.

Reference

Phillips, P., and Burkett, H. *ROI on a Shoestring*. Alexandria, Va.: ASTD, 2001.

ROI Quiz

True or false? Please choose the answer you feel is correct.

	True	False
1. The ROI Methodology generates just one data item, expressed as a percentage.	☐	☐
2. A program with monetary benefits of $200,000 and costs of $100,000 translates into a 200% ROI.	☐	☐
3. The ROI Methodology is a tool to strengthen organizations and improve processes.	☐	☐
4. After reviewing a detailed ROI impact study, senior executives will usually require ROI studies on all programs.	☐	☐
5. ROI studies should be conducted very selectively, usually involving 5–10% of programs.	☐	☐
6. While it may be a rough estimate, it is always possible to isolate the effects of a program on impact data.	☐	☐
7. A program costing $100 per participant, designed to teach basic skills on job-related software, is an ideal program for an ROI impact study.	☐	☐
8. Data can always be credibly converted to monetary value.	☐	☐
9. The ROI Methodology contains too many complicated formulas.	☐	☐
10. The ROI Methodology can be implemented for about 3–5% of my budget.	☐	☐

	True	False
11. ROI is not future-oriented; it reflects only past performance.	☐	☐
12. It is not possible to measure ROI for soft-skills programs.	☐	☐
13. When an ROI impact study conducted on an existing program shows a negative ROI, the client is usually already aware of the program's weaknesses.	☐	☐
14. The best time to consider an ROI evaluation is three months after the program is completed.	☐	☐
15. In the early stages of implementation, the ROI Methodology is a process improvement tool and not a performance evaluation tool for the staff.	☐	☐
16. If senior executives are not asking for ROI, there is no need to pursue the ROI Methodology.	☐	☐

Quiz Answers

1. False

2. False

3. True

4. False

5. True

6. True

7. False

8. False

9. False

10. True

11. False

12. False

13. True

14. False

15. True

16. False

So, how did you do?

Now that the answers to the quiz have been given, see how you fared. Tally your score. Look at the interpretations that follow. What is your ROI acumen?

Number of Correct Responses	
14–16	You could be an ROI consultant!
10–13	You could be a speaker at the next ROI conference.
7–9	You need a copy of a thick ROI book.
4–6	You need to attend a two-day ROI workshop.
1–3	You need to attend the ROI certification.

6

Planning for Evaluation

The first part of this book presented the fundamentals of the ROI Methodology. Understanding the theoretical basis of the process is important, for it is the foundation of a successful, sustainable practice. This book now concludes by introducing the first step in the process. This step, evaluation planning, is the foundation of a successful ROI evaluation study.

Establishing Purpose and Feasibility

The first step in planning an evaluation is identifying the purpose and feasibility of conducting a comprehensive evaluation, including ROI.

Purpose

A clear evaluation purpose helps keep the evaluator and the team on track, preventing the project from becoming too overwhelming. Purpose keeps the evaluation focused on the "why," providing a basis for using the data once they are generated. All too often, an evaluation is conducted without understanding the reason for the process. Therefore, the raw data sit for days and months before the evaluator analyzes them to obtain the results. Defining the purpose of the evaluation helps determine the scope of the evaluation project. It drives the type of data to be collected as well as the type of data collection instruments used. Evaluation purposes range from demonstrating the value of a particular program to boosting the credibility of an entire function or department.

Make Decisions About Programs

Decisions are made every day, with and without evaluation data. But with evaluation data, departments can better influence those decisions. Evaluation data can aid decision making about a program prior to the launch of the program, for example, when ROI is forecast for a pilot program. Once the results of the evaluation are known, department leaders can decide whether to pursue the program further.

Evaluation data can help the staff make decisions about internal development issues. For example, reaction (Level 1) data provide information that helps determine the extent to which facilitators need additional skill building. Learning (Level 2) data can help the project leader decide whether an additional learning activity will better emphasize a skill that has been left undeveloped. Application (Level 3) data reveal the extent to which barriers are preventing employees from applying knowledge and skills on the job. Impact (Level 4) and ROI (Level 5) data help senior managers and executives decide whether they will continue investing in certain programs. The five levels of evaluation provide different types of data that influence different decisions.

Improve Programs and Processes

One of the most important purposes for generating comprehensive data with the ROI Methodology is improvement of programs and processes. As data are generated, the programs under evaluation can be adjusted so that future programs will be more effective than those that did not fare well according to the data. Reviewing evaluation data during early stages of the program or initiative allows the staff to apply additional tools and processes to support the program.

Evaluation data can help a function improve its accountability processes. By consistently evaluating programs, the function will find ways to collect and analyze data more efficiently through technology or through the use of experts within the organization. Evaluation will also cause the staff to view its programs and processes in a different light, asking such questions as, "Will this prove valuable to the organization?" "Can the organization get the same results for less cost?" and, "How can the staff influence the manager to better support this program?"

Demonstrate Program Value

The ultimate purpose of conducting comprehensive evaluation is to show the value of programs—specifically their economic value. However, when individual programs are considered for evaluation, the question is often "the value to whom?"

Value usually does not have one definition within an organization. Similar to the way learning occurs at the societal, community, team, and individual levels, value is defined from the perspectives of different stakeholders:

- Is a program valuable to those involved?

- Is a program valuable to the system that supports it?

- Is a program economically valuable?

The different definitions of value come from three perspectives. These perspectives are put into context by comparing them to the five-level ROI framework. Figure 6.1 presents these perspectives. The consumer perspective represents the extent to which those directly involved in the program react positively and acquire some level of knowledge or skills from their participation. The system perspective represents the supporting elements within the organization that make the program work. The economic perspective represents the extent to which the knowledge or skills that are transferred to the job positively affect key business measures. When appropriate,

Figure 6.1. Value Perspectives

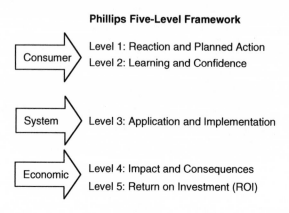

these benefits are converted to monetary values and compared to the costs of the program to calculate an economic value, ROI.

Consumer Perspective. Consumers are those who have an immediate connection with a program. Facilitators, designers, developers, and participants represent consumers. Value to this group is represented at Levels 1 and 2. Data from those levels provide feedback so that the staff can make immediate changes to a program as well as decide where developmental needs exist. The data also provide the participants with information on what the group thought about the program as well as how much success they had in learning the knowledge and skills taught in the program. Specific measures—those representing use of knowledge gained—are often used to predict the application of knowledge and skills that will occur when participants return to their jobs.

System Perspective. The system represents the people and functions that support programs within an organization. This group includes participants' managers, participants' peers, program team members, executives, and other support functions. While Level 3 data provide evidence of participants' application of their newly acquired knowledge and skills, the greatest value in evaluating at this level is determining the extent to which the system supported learning transfer and application of the program. This is determined by the barriers and enablers identified through the Level 3 evaluation.

Economic Perspective. The economic perspective is important for the client—the person or group funding the program. While certainly the participants' managers are interested in whether the program influenced business outcomes and may be interested in the ROI, the client—usually senior management—makes the financial investment in the program. Levels 4 and 5 provide data that show the economic value of the investment.

Feasibility

Program evaluations have multiple purposes. Even when a program is being evaluated at Level 5 in order to aid funding decisions, Level 1 data are still needed to improve delivery and design of the program. This is one reason that lower-level evaluations are conducted more often than higher-level ones. Other drivers that determine the feasibility of evaluating programs include validation of program objectives, availability of data, and appropriateness of the ROI Methodology for the organization.

Validation of Program Objectives

Program objectives are the fundamental basis for evaluation. Program objectives drive the design and development of a program and define how to measure success. Program objectives define what the program is intended to do, how to measure participant achievement, and a support system for application of the learning on the job. Evaluation provides data to determine whether these objectives have been met. Too often, however, too little emphasis is placed on developing objectives and defining their measures.

Availability of Data

Is information available that will determine whether the objectives have been met? The availability of Level 1 and Level 2 data is rarely a concern. Simply ask program participants for their opinion, test them, or facilitate role-playing or exercises to assess their overall understanding, and the data are there. Level 3 data are often obtained through follow-ups with participants or their managers, peers, or direct reports. The challenge is availability of Level 4 data. Are measures being monitored on a routine basis? If not, who or where is the best source of this information and how can it be collected?

Appropriateness for ROI Measurement

Program objectives and data availability are key drivers in determining the feasibility of evaluating a program's ROI. However, it is good to keep in mind that some programs are just not appropriate for an ROI evaluation.

The issue to consider in assessing the appropriateness of a program for ROI is whether it meets specific criteria. An inexpensive program offered on a one-time basis is usually not suitable for ROI. Why invest resources in conducting such a comprehensive evaluation on a program for which the data will serve no valuable or ongoing purpose? Basic skill building—for example, instruction in basic computer skills—is not always suitable for ROI. Sometimes, you just want to know that participants know how to do something rather than what impact their doing it has on the organization. Orientation or on-boarding programs are not always suitable for a full ROI evaluation—especially entry-level programs in which participants are just beginning their professional career.

Defining Program Objectives

Before evaluation begins, program objectives must be developed. Program objectives are linked to needs assessment. When a problem or opportunity is identified, needs assessment begins. Assessments are conducted to determine exactly what the problem is, how on-the-job performance change can resolve the problem, what knowledge or skills need to be acquired to change on-the-job performance, and how best to present the solution so that those involved, the consumers, can acquire the knowledge and skills to change performance and solve the business problem. From this point, program objectives are developed to guide program designers and developers, provide guidance to facilitators, establish goals for participants, and set up a framework for evaluators.

Program objectives reflect the same five-level ROI framework used in categorizing evaluation data (see Chapter One). When you are writing program objectives, the key is to be specific in identifying measures of success. All too often, very broad program objectives are stated. While broad objectives are acceptable in the initial phases of program design, it is specific measures of success that drive results and serve as the basis for evaluation.

Reaction Objectives

Level 1 objectives are critical because they describe expected immediate and long-term satisfaction with a program. They describe issues that are important to the success of the program, including facilitation, relevance and importance of content, logistics, and intended use of knowledge and skills. But there has been criticism of the use of Level 1 overall satisfaction as a measure of success. The overuse of the overall satisfaction measure has led many organizations to make funding decisions based on whether participants like a program; but later such organizations may find that the data were misleading.

Level 1 objectives should identify important, measurable issues rather than esoteric indicators that provide limited useful information. Level 1 objectives should be attitude-based, clearly worded, and specific. Level 1 objectives specify that the participants have changed their thinking or perceptions as a result of the program and underscore the link between attitude and the success of the program. While Level 1 objectives represent a satisfaction index from the consumer's perspective, these objectives should also be capable of predicting program success. Given these criteria, Level 1 objectives must be represented by specific measures of success.

A good predictor of the application of knowledge and skills is participants' perception of the relevance of a program's content. Thus, an example of a Level 1 objective might be

- At the end of the program, participants indicate that the program content is relevant to their job.

A question remains, however: "How will evaluators know that they have achieved this objective?" A more specific objective is

- At the end of the program, 80 percent of participants rate the program's relevance at 4.5 out of 5 on a Likert scale.

Those who are research-oriented might want to take the objective a step further by defining *relevance*. Relevance may be defined as

- Knowledge and skills that participants can immediately apply in their work

- Knowledge and skills reflective of participants' day-to-day work activities

If this is the case, the measures of success (the objectives) can be even more detailed:

- At the end of the program, 80 percent of the participants indicate that they can *immediately apply the*

knowledge and skills in their work and indicate this by
rating this measure at 4.5 out of 5 on a Likert scale.

- At the end of the program, 80 percent of the participants view the knowledge and skills as *reflective of their
  day-to-day work activities* and indicate this by rating this
  measure 4.5 out of 5 on a Likert scale.

The ratings on these two measures can be reported individually
or combined to create a relevance index.

Overall satisfaction is often referred to as a measure of how
much participants liked the cookies offered during a program or the
shrimp at a conference. For example, recent analysis of a comprehensive Level 1 end-of-course questionnaire showed that participants viewed the program as less than relevant and not useful and
that they had little intention of applying what they had learned.
Mean scores were as follows:

- Knowledge and skills presented are relevant to my job.
  (2.8 out of 5)

- Knowledge and skills presented will be useful to my
  work. (2.6 out of 5)

- I intend to use what I learned in this course. (2.2 out
  of 5)

Surprisingly, however, respondents scored the overall satisfaction measure, "I am satisfied with the program," 4.6 out of 5. Perhaps
they were rating the cookies.

Breaking down objectives to specific measures provides a clearer
picture of success. However, it also lengthens your Level 1 data
collection instrument and requires more analysis. The question to
ask is, "Is this detail in my measures really needed?" For a program
planned for an ROI evaluation, no. Simple but specific Level 1

objectives and measures are sufficient when evaluating a program to the ROI level. Conserve your resources for the more challenging tasks of Level 4 and Level 5 evaluation. Exhibit 6.1 summarizes the guidelines for Level 1 objectives.

Learning Objectives

Organizations are increasingly interested in evaluating the acquisition of knowledge and skills. Drivers of the heightened interest include an increase in the number of learning organizations, emphasis on intellectual capital, and more use of certification as a discriminator in the employee selection process. Given this, Level 2 objectives should be well defined.

Learning objectives communicate the expected outcomes of the program; they describe competent performance that should result from the program. The best learning objectives describe behaviors that are observable and measurable. Like reaction objectives, learning objectives are outcome-based. Clearly worded and specific, they spell out what the participant must do as a result of the skills and knowledge learned during the program.

A typical learning objective might be

- At the end of the program, participants will be able to implement Microsoft Word.

Sounds reasonable, but what does successful implementation look like? How will you know the objective has been achieved? Measures are needed to evaluate the success of learning, such as:

- At the end of the program, participants will be able to demonstrate to the facilitator the following applications of Microsoft Word within a ten-minute time period and with zero errors:
  - File, Save As, Save As Web Page

Exhibit 6.1. Guidelines for Reaction and Satisfaction Objectives

Reaction objectives are critical in this measurement chain because they

- Describe expected immediate and long-term satisfaction.
- Describe issues that are important to the success of the program.
- Provide a basis for evaluating the beginning of the measurement chain of impact.
- Place emphasis on planned action, if feasible.

The best reaction objectives

- Identify issues that are important and measurable.
- Are attitude-based, clearly worded, and specific.
- Specify that the participant has changed in thinking or perception as a result of the program.
- Underscore the link between attitude and the success of the program.
- Represent a satisfaction index from key stakeholders.
- Predict program success.

Key questions:

- How relevant is this program?
- How important is this program?
- Are the facilitators effective?
- How appropriate is this program?
- Is this new information?
- Is this program rewarding?
- Will you implement this program?
- Will you use the concepts or advice?
- What would keep you from implementing the objectives of this program?
- Would you recommend this program to others?

- Formatting, including font, paragraph, background, and themes
- Insert tables, add columns and rows, and delete columns and rows

Exhibit 6.2 summarizes the guidelines for Level 2 objectives.

Exhibit 6.2. Guidelines for Learning Objectives

Learning objectives are critical to measuring learning because they
- Communicate expected outcomes from instruction.
- Describe competent performance that should be the result of learning.
- Provide a basis for evaluating learning.
- Focus on learning for participants.

The best learning objectives

- Describe behaviors that are observable and measurable.
- Are outcome-based, clearly worded, and specific.
- Specify what the learner must do as a result of the learning.
- Have three components:
  1. *Performance:* what the learner will be able to do at the end of the program
  2. *Conditions:* circumstances under which the learner will perform the task
  3. *Criteria:* degree or level of proficiency that is necessary to perform the job

Three types of learning objectives are

1. *Awareness:* familiarity with terms, concepts, and processes
2. *Knowledge:* general understanding of concepts and processes
3. *Performance:* ability to demonstrate the skill (at least at a basic level)

Application Objectives

Whereas learning objectives describe what participants can do, Level 3 objectives describe what participants are expected to do to implement the program. Application objectives describe the expected intermediate outcomes of the program. They describe competent performance that should occur as a result of the program and provide the basis for evaluating on-the-job performance changes. The emphasis is on applying what was learned.

The best Level 3 objectives identify behaviors that are observable and measurable; in addition, they are outcome-based, clearly worded, specific, and spell out what the participant has changed as a result of the program.

A typical application objective might read like this:

- Participants will use effective meeting behaviors.

Again, specifics may be needed in order to define success. What are effective meeting behaviors, and to what degree should participants use those skills? Here are some examples of more specific objectives:

- Returning to their job, participants will develop a detailed agenda outlining the specific topics to be covered for 100 percent of their meetings.

- Participants will establish meeting ground rules at the beginning of 100 percent of their meetings.

- Participants will follow up on meeting action items within three days following 100 percent of their meetings.

Two important elements of Level 3 evaluation are barriers and enablers. Does the system support learning? Barriers to application as well as supporting elements (enablers) need to be examined. It is important to collect data about these issues so that corrective action can be taken when evidence of a problem exists. How can issues outside the program be controlled? For example, what should be done if participants indicate that their manager prevents them from applying newly acquired knowledge? Through the evaluation process, data are collected that prepare evaluators to engage in dialogue with managers. Bringing managers into the fold and asking them for help gets them involved in the process and helps gain their support. One example might be informing a group of managers that there is evidence that some managers do not support the project and that the group's advice on how to remedy the situation is needed. Initiating such a dialogue gives some control to evaluators.

Comprehensive assessment at Level 3 provides the tools to begin a dialogue with all stakeholders. Through such dialogue, managers and colleagues in other departments may admit, for example, that they do not understand the role of the program. Exhibit 6.3 summarizes the guidelines for Level 3 objectives.

Impact Objectives

Success in achieving Level 4 objectives is critical when a positive ROI is desired. Impact objectives provide the basis for measuring the application of skills and knowledge while placing emphasis on bottom-line results. The best impact objectives contain measures that are linked to the skills and knowledge in the program and are easily collected. Impact objectives are results-based, clearly worded, and specific. They spell out what a participant has accomplished in their business unit as a result of the program.

Impact objectives involving hard data are output, quality, cost, and time. Impact measures involving soft data are customer service, work climate, and attitudes.

Exhibit 6.3. Guidelines for Application Objectives

Application objectives are critical to measuring application of skills and knowledge because they

- Describe expected intermediate outcomes.
- Describe competent performance that should be the result of the program.
- Provide a basis for evaluation of on-the-job performance changes.
- Place emphasis on applying what was learned.

The best application objectives

- Identify behaviors that are observable and measurable.
- Are outcome-based, clearly worded, and specific.
- Specify what the participant has changed or will change as a result of the training.
- May have three components:
  1. *Performance:* what the participant has changed or accomplished at a specified follow-up time after the program
  2. *Conditions:* circumstances under which the participant performed the task
  3. *Criteria:* degree or level of proficiency at which the task or job was performed

Two types of application objectives are

- *Knowledge-based:* general use of concepts and processes
- *Behavior-based:* demonstration of the skill (at least at a basic level)

Key questions:

- What new or improved knowledge will be applied on the job?
- What new or improved skill will be applied on the job?
- What will be the frequency of skill application?
- What new tasks will be performed?
- What new steps will be implemented?
- What new action items will be implemented?
- What new procedures will be implemented or changed?
- What new guidelines will be implemented or changed?
- What new processes will be implemented or changed?

For example, the beer industry is losing market share to high-end spirits. Coors implements a marketing strategy that includes new ads showing a sleek, silver Love Train delivering Coors to upscale partygoers (Howard, 2005). The impact objective and measure of success might look like this:

- Increase market share of young professionals by 10 percent within nine months of new ad launch

In another example, a large multinational computer manufacturer prides itself on the quality of the computer systems it sells and the service provided when problems arise. The company makes it easy for purchasers to secure assistance by selling lucrative warranties on all of its products. One particular system, the X-1350, comes with a three-year warranty that includes "gold standard" technical support for only an additional $105.

In the past year, the number of calls to repair contractors has increased, particularly in regard to the X-1350. This increase is costing the company not only money but also customer satisfaction. A new program is implemented to improve the quality of the computer. The impact objective and specific measures of success are

- Reduce the number of warranty claims on the X-1350 by 10 percent within six months after the start of the program

- Improve by 10 percent the overall customer satisfaction with the quality of the X-1350 as indicated by a customer satisfaction survey taken six months after the start of the program

- Achieve top box scores on product quality measures included in an industry quality survey

Exhibit 6.4. Guidelines for Impact Objectives

Impact objectives are critical to measuring business performance because they

- Describe expected outcomes.
- Describe business unit performance that should be the result of a program.
- Provide a basis for measuring the consequences of application of skills and knowledge.
- Place emphasis on achieving bottom-line results.

The best impact objectives

- Contain measures that are linked to the skills and knowledge of the program.
- Describe measures that are easily collected.
- Are results-based, clearly worded, and specific.
- Specify what the participants have accomplished in their business unit as a result of the program.

Four types of impact objectives involving hard data are

- Output-focused
- Quality-focused
- Cost-focused
- Time-focused

Three common types of impact objectives involving soft data are

- Customer service–focused
- Work climate–focused
- Work habit–focused

Exhibit 6.4 summarizes the guidelines for Level 4 objectives.

ROI Objectives

Level 5 objectives target the specific economic return anticipated when an investment is made in a program. This objective defines *good* when someone asks, "What is a good ROI?" When you are setting a target ROI, there are four options. The first is to set the target ROI at the same level as the desired ROI for capital investments in plant, equipment, and buildings. Targeting the same ROI for programs and capital investments is not uncommon. Many groups use this approach to ensure a link with operations. To establish this target, finance and accounting should be asked what the average return is for other investments.

Another option for establishing ROI objectives is to raise the bar for the program, setting the target ROI at a higher level than for other investments. Because programs affect so many and contribute so much to an organization, expecting a higher-than-normal ROI is not unreasonable.

Some organizations are satisfied with another option: a 0 percent ROI—that is, breaking even. Breaking even means that the organization got its investment back; for example, if an organization spent $50,000 on a program and the benefits were $50,000, there was no gain, but the investment was returned. Many organizations—such as public sector, nonprofit, community, and faith-based organizations—value the break-even ROI.

A fourth way to set an ROI objective is to ask the client. The client is the person or group that is funding the program. This person or group may be willing to invest in a program for a specific return on investment. Exhibit 6.5 summarizes the guidelines for establishing a Level 5 target.

Exhibit 6.5. Guidelines for ROI Objectives

Level 5 objectives are established by considering the following:

- Current level of return on capital investments
- A percentage return higher than typical for investment returns on capital equipment
- Break-even
- Client needs and expectations

Developing the Planning Documents

Three basic documents must be created when you are planning an ROI evaluation: a data collection plan, an ROI analysis plan, and a project plan. If you are thorough in completing these documents, your ROI evaluation plan will be well under way. Once they are completed, the client should sign off on the plan for evaluation. By taking this important step, the client buys into and shows confidence in the approach.

Data Collection Plan

The data collection plan lays the initial groundwork for the ROI study. Table 6.1 presents an example of a completed data collection plan. The columns of this plan hold the answers to several questions.

What Do You Ask?

The answers to this question lie in the program objectives and their respective measures. Specific measurable objectives and measures of success are the basis of the questions you will ask. When broad objectives are developed, the measures must be clearly described so that you will know when success is achieved.

How Do You Ask?

How you will ask for the information depends on a variety of issues, including the resources available for data collection. Level 1 data are typically collected by means of an end-of-course questionnaire. To collect Level 2 data, tests, role-playing, self-assessments, and facilitator assessments are used. Obtaining application data (Level 3) and impact data (Level 4) is the most challenging. However, a variety of options are available, including questionnaires, focus groups, interviews, action plans, and performance monitoring. These options provide flexibility and ensure that a lack of data collection methods is not a barrier to assessing the application and impact of a program.

Table 6.1. Completed Data Collection Plan

			Data Collection Method and Instruments	Data Sources	Timing	Responsibility
Program: Absenteeism Reduction				**Responsibility:** Jack Phillips	**Date:** January 15	

Data Collection Plan—Metro Transit Authority   Evaluation Purpose:

Level	Broad Program Objective(s)	Measures	Data Collection Method and Instruments	Data Sources	Timing	Responsibility
1	**REACTION AND PLANNED ACTION** • Positive employee reaction to the no fault policy	• Positive reaction from employees	• Feedback questionnaire	• Employees	• At the end of employee meetings	• Supervisors
2	**LEARNING** • Employee understanding of the policy	• Score of at least 70 on posttest	• True/false test	• Employees	• At the end of employee meetings	• Supervisors

3	APPLICATION AND IMPLEMENTATION				
	1. Effective and consistent implementation and enforcement of the program	1. Supervisors' response on program's influence	1. & 2. Follow-up questionnaire to supervisors (two sample groups)	1. & 2. Supervisors	1. & 2. Following employee meetings, sample one group at three months and another group at six months	1., 2., & 3. HR program coordinator
	2. Little or no adverse reaction from current employees toward no fault policy	2. Employee complaints and union cooperation			2. Three months and six months after implementation	
	3. Use the new screening process		3. Sample review of interview and selection records	3. Company records		

(Continued)

Table 6.1. Completed Data Collection Plan (*Continued*)

Level	Broad Program Objective(s)	Measures	Data Collection Method and Instruments	Data Sources	Timing	Responsibility
4	**IMPACT**					
	1. Reduce driver absenteeism at least 2% during first year	1. Absenteeism	1. Monitor absenteeism	1. Company records	1. Monitor monthly; analyze one year before and one year after implementation	1., 2., & 3. HR program coordinator
	2. Maintain present level of job satisfaction as new policy is implemented	2. Employee satisfaction	2. Follow-up questionnaire to supervisors	2. Supervisors	2. Three months and six months after employee meetings	
	3. Improved customer service and satisfaction with reduction in schedule delays	3. Impact of delays on customer service	3. Monitor bus schedule delays	3. Dispatch records	3. Monthly	
5	**ROI**					
	Target ROI 25%	*Comments:*				

Whom Do You Ask?

Data sources are critical. Only the most credible sources should be used, and sometimes, maximizing credibility means using multiple sources to corroborate the data. The more credible the sources of the data, the more reliable the data are. The only constraint is the expense of going to multiple sources.

When Do You Ask?

The timing of data collection is critical, and getting it right is sometimes a challenge. Enough time must pass to allow new behaviors to become routine, but not so long that participants might forget how they developed the new behavior. Also, enough time must pass to allow results to occur, yet most executives are not willing to wait a year. Therefore, a time must be chosen with which all stakeholders are comfortable.

Who Asks?

Who will be responsible for each step in the data collection process? Typically, the facilitator or project leader collects data at Levels 1 and 2. For the higher levels of evaluation, representatives of the evaluation team are assigned specific roles, including data collection. A person or team is assigned the task of developing the data collection instrument and administering it. This task includes developing a strategy to ensure an adequate response rate.

ROI Analysis Plan

The second evaluation planning document is the ROI analysis plan (see Table 6.2 for an example). The ROI analysis plan identifies several elements.

Methods for Isolating the Effects of the Program

The technique that will be used to isolate the effects of the program must be chosen. Typically, the method of isolation is the same for all measures. Sometimes, some measures can be isolated through

Table 6.2. Completed ROI Analysis Plan

ROI Analysis Plan—Metro Transit Authority

Program: Absenteeism Reduction   **Responsibility:** Jack Phillips   **Date:** January 15

Data Items (Usually Level 4)	Methods for Isolating the Effects of the Program or Process	Methods for Converting Data to Monetary Values	Cost Categories	Intangible Benefits	Communication Targets for Final Report	Other Influences and Issues	Comments
1. Absenteeism	1. Trend line analysis and supervisor estimates	1. Wages and benefits and standard values	**Screening Process** • Development • Interviewer preparation • Administration • Materials **No Fault Policy** • Development • Implementation • Materials **Evaluation**	• Sustain employee satisfaction • Improve employee morale • Improve customer satisfaction • Fewer disruptive bottlenecks in transportation grid • Ease of implementation by supervisors	• Senior management • Managers and supervisors • Union representatives • HR staff	• Concern about whether supervisors are providing consistent administration • Partner with union reps on how to communicate results of study to employees	
2. Employee job satisfaction	2. Supervisor estimates	N/A					
3. Bus schedule delays (influence on customer satisfaction)	3. Management estimates	N/A					

the use of a control group, but other measures have to use another technique.

Methods for Converting Data to Monetary Values

The ROI analysis plan identifies the methods for converting impact measures to monetary values. In some cases, a measure will purposely not be converted to a monetary value.

Cost Categories

This section includes all the costs of the program. These costs include needs assessment, program design and development, program delivery, evaluation costs, and some amount for overhead and administrative costs for the people and processes that support the program. Each cost category is listed on the ROI analysis plan.

Intangible Benefits

Not all measures will be converted to monetary values. The measures that are not converted to monetary values are considered intangible benefits. Any Level 4 measures that are not converted to monetary values should be moved to this column. Also, this column includes any anticipated intangible benefits that might occur as a result of the program.

Communication Targets for the Final Report

In many cases, organizations plan their communication targets in detail. During the evaluation planning phase, the audiences to whom the final report will be submitted should be identified. Four key audiences always get a copy or summary of the report: participants, staff, participants' supervisors, and client.

Other Application Influences and Issues

This section provides an opportunity to anticipate any issues that might occur during the program that might have a negative effect (as well as ones that might have no effect) on the identified measures. This column can also be used to list issues that might have a negative effect on the evaluation process.

Comments

The final section of the ROI analysis plan is for comments. Notes can be included to remind the evaluation team of key issues. Comments about the potential success or failure of the program can be listed in this column as well as reminders of specific tasks to be conducted by the evaluation team.

The importance of planning the data collection for an ROI analysis cannot be stressed enough. Carefully planning, in detail, what will be asked, how it will be asked, who will be asked, when to ask, and who will do the asking, along with the key steps in the ROI analysis, will ensure successful implementation. In addition, having clients sign off on the plans will ensure support when the evaluation results are presented.

Project Plan

After the data collection plan and the ROI analysis plan have been developed, the next step is to develop a simple project plan. This plan is essentially a timeline of the major steps, activities, and milestones in implementing the program and conducting an ROI evaluation. It should be simple, perhaps using whatever project management tool is typically used in any organization. It begins with the planning stage and ends when all the steps are completed and the data are communicated to the appropriate audiences. Some add another step and track adjustments and changes that are made after the results have been communicated. Exhibit 6.6 shows a simple, completed project plan.

Exhibit 6.6. Project Plan

	FEB	MAR	APR	MAY	JUN	JUL	AUG	SEP
Decision to conduct ROI study	▓							
Evaluation planning complete	▓							
Instruments designed	▓							
Instruments pilot-tested		▓						
Data collected from Group A		▓	▓					
Data collected from Group B				▓				
Data collected from Group C					▓			
Data tabulation preliminary summary					▓			
Analysis conducted						▓		
Report written						▓		
Report printed						▓		
Results communicated							▓	
Improvements initiated							▓	
Implementation complete								▓

Conducting the Planning Meeting

The evaluation planning meeting is crucial to developing the plans described in this chapter. In most situations, it is a formal meeting with specific individuals involved, an agenda, and a strategy for success.

Who Should Be Involved

Essentially, the people who know the program or project best should be involved: the person who owns the program, the individual who will design it, the person who analyzed the initial need for the program, the facilitator, and a person in the business unit who understands the business data. Perhaps one of the most important individuals is the subject matter expert who understands the content of the program. If it's appropriate and feasible, having these typical participants at the meeting may be useful. Each may uncover issues not seen by the others.

Agenda

The agenda should be simple and basic, and it should include the following items:

- Explanation of the purpose of the program

- Finalized or adjusted objectives

- Completed data collection plan

- Completed ROI analysis plan

- Completed project plan

The meeting can usually be accomplished (1) in a day for individuals who are just beginning to use the ROI Methodology, (2) in about a half day as confidence builds and comfort and expertise increases, or (3) with help from some technology to support data entry, in two hours.

Factors for Success

The evaluation planning meeting must be successful because it is the beginning point of the process, and all the key decisions about the evaluation, methodology, and approach are defined within it. Several factors can contribute to success. First, the most credible sources must either attend the meeting or be available to the group. Full access to data must be available, and in some cases, the data should be brought to the meeting. All the issues that might affect the program's success must be covered completely during this meeting. It should move quickly to save the precious time of the group. The output of the meeting should be considered a draft, not final; the planning documents may go through several iterations before they are finalized. At the end of the meeting, the key sponsor of the project or program should sign the planning documents, stating that he or she approves and understands the approaches that are being taken. This can avoid confusion, frustration, and disappointment later in the project or, even worse, when the results are presented.

Identifying Data Sources

When considering the possible sources for data collection, six categories are easily defined. Each source will have its advantages and disadvantages.

Organizational Performance Records

The most useful and credible data source for an ROI analysis is the records and reports of the organization. Whether individualized or group-based, the records reflect performance in a work unit, department, division, region, or the entire organization. Organizational records can include all types of measures, which are usually available in abundance throughout the organization. Collecting data from performance records is preferred for Level 4 evaluation because the data usually reflect business impact data and are relatively easy to obtain. However, sloppy record keeping by some organizations may make locating some data difficult.

Participants

The most widely used data source for an ROI analysis is program participants. Participants are frequently asked about their reactions and planned actions, the extent of their learning, and how they have applied the skills and knowledge on the job. Sometimes, they are asked to explain the impact of those actions. Participants are a rich source of data at Levels 1, 2, 3, and 4. They are credible because they are the individuals who were involved in the program and who achieved the performance. Also, they are often the most knowledgeable about the processes and other influencing factors. The challenge is finding an effective and efficient method of capturing data consistently.

Participants' Managers

Another important source of data is the immediate managers of the program participants. This group will often have a vested interest in the evaluation process because they approved the participants' involvement in the program. In many situations, they observe the participants as they attempt to apply the knowledge and skills acquired through the program. Consequently, they can report on the successes linked to the program as well as the difficulties and problems associated with application. Although manager input is usually best for Level 3 data, it can be useful for Level 4. However, the managers must maintain objectivity and give an unbiased assessment of the program participants.

Participants' Direct Reports

In situations in which supervisors and managers are involved in a program, their direct reports can provide information about perceived changes in observable behavior that have occurred since the program. Input from direct reports is appropriate for Level 3 data (behavior) but not necessarily Level 4 (impact). Collecting data from a manager's direct reports can be very helpful and instructive; however, it is often avoided because of potential biases that can enter into the feedback process.

Team or Peer Group

Individuals who are teammates of the participant or who occupy peer-level positions within the organization are another potential source of data for a few types of programs. In these situations, peers provide input on perceived behavioral changes of participants (Level 3). This source of data is more appropriate when all team members participate in the program and, consequently, when they report on the collective efforts of the group or behavioral changes of specific individuals. Because of the subjective nature of this process and the lack of opportunity to fully evaluate the application of skills, this source of data is somewhat limited.

Internal and External Groups

In some situations, internal or external groups, such as project staff, program facilitators, expert observers, or external consultants, may provide input on the success of individuals when they learn and apply the skills and knowledge involved in a program. Sometimes, expert observers or assessors may be used to measure learning (Level 2). This source may also be useful for on-the-job observation (Level 3) after the program has been completed. Collecting data from internal or external groups has limited uses. Because internal groups may have a vested interest in the outcome of evaluation, their input may not be very credible.

Final Thoughts

This chapter detailed the entire ROI evaluation planning process. From establishing the purpose of the program to identifying data sources, evaluation planning is the critical first step for successful programs. Each step of the planning process must be completed so that essential data are collected at the right time, analyzed, and reported to the right people. Without this evaluation framework in place—from the beginning—the program is likely doomed to fail. Once the planning process has been established and a data collection plan, ROI analysis plan, and project plan have been signed by all stakeholders, the program and the data collection can begin.

Reference

Howard, T. "Brewers Get into the Spirits of Marketing." *USA Today*, May 16, 2005, p. 18.

Appendix: Resources

The Bottomline on ROI, by Patricia Pulliam Phillips. Atlanta, Ga.: Center for Effective Performance, 2002.

The Chief Learning Officer, by Tamar Elkeles and Jack J. Phillips. Woburn, Mass. Butterworth-Heinemann, 2006.

The Consultant's Scorecard, by Jack J. Phillips. New York: McGraw-Hill, 2000.

Handbook of Training Evaluation and Measurement Methods, by Jack J. Phillips. (3rd ed.) Woburn, Mass.: Butterworth-Heinemann, 1997.

How to Measure Training Results, by Jack J. Phillips and Ron Drew Stone. New York: McGraw-Hill, 2002.

The Human Resources Scorecard, by Jack J. Phillips, Patricia Pulliam Phillips, and Ron Drew Stone. Woburn, Mass.: Butterworth-Heinemann, 2001.

The Leadership Scorecard, by Jack J. Phillips and Lynn Schmidt. Woburn, Mass.: Butterworth-Heinemann, 2004.

Make Training Evaluation Work, by Jack J. Phillips, Patricia Pulliam Phillips, and Tony Krucky Hodges. Alexandria, Va.: ASTD, 2004.

The Project Management Scorecard, by Jack J. Phillips, Timothy W. Bothell, and G. Lynne Snead. Woburn, Mass.: Butterworth-Heinemann, 2002.

Proving the Value of HR: How and Why to Measure ROI, by Jack J. Phillips and Patricia Pulliam Phillips. Alexandria, Va.: Society for Human Resource Management, 2005.

Proving the Value of Meetings and Events, by Jack J. Phillips, Monica Myhill, and James B. McDonough. Birmingham, Ala.: ROI Institute and MPI, 2007.

Return on Investment in Training and Performance Improvement Programs, by Jack J. Phillips. (2nd ed.) Woburn, Mass.: Butterworth-Heinemann, 2003.

Return on Investment (ROI) Basics, by Patricia Pulliam Phillips and Jack J. Phillips. Alexandria, Va.: ASTD, 2005.

ROI at Work: Best-Practice Case Studies from the Real World, by Jack J. Phillips and Patricia Pulliam Phillips. Alexandria, Va.: ASTD, 2005.

The ROI Field Book, by Patricia Pulliam Phillips, Jack J. Phillips, Ron D. Stone, and Holly Burkett. Woburn, Mass.: Butterworth-Heinemann, 2006.

Show Me the Money: How to Determine ROI in People, Projects, and Programs, by Jack J. Phillips and Patricia Pulliam Phillips. San Francisco: Berrett-Koehler, 2007.

The Value of Learning, by Patricia Pulliam Phillips and Jack J. Phillips. San Francisco: Pfeiffer, 2007.

Index

About the Authors

Patricia Pulliam Phillips, Ph.D., is president of the ROI Institute, Inc., the leading source of ROI competency building, implementation support, networking, and research. She supports organizations in their efforts to build accountability into their training, human resources, and performance improvement programs with a primary focus on building accountability in public sector organizations. She helps organizations implement the ROI Methodology in countries around the world, including South Africa, Singapore, Japan, New Zealand, Australia, Italy, Turkey, France, Germany, Canada, and the United States.

In 1997, after a thirteen-year career in the electrical utility industry, she embraced the ROI Methodology by committing herself to ongoing research and practice. To this end, Phillips has implemented the ROI Methodology in private sector and public sector organizations. She has conducted ROI impact studies of programs in leadership development, sales, new-hire orientation, human performance improvement, K–12 educator development, National Board Certification mentoring for educators, and faculty fellowship. Phillips is currently expanding her interest in public sector accountability by applying the ROI Methodology in community- and faith-based initiatives.

Phillips teaches others to implement the ROI Methodology through the ROI certification process, as a facilitator for ASTD's

ROI and Measuring and Evaluating Learning workshops, and as an adjunct professor for graduate-level evaluation courses. She speaks on the topic of ROI at conferences such as ASTD's International Conference and Exposition and the International Society for Performance Improvement's International Conference.

Phillips's academic accomplishments include a master's degree in public and private management and a Ph.D. degree in international development. She is certified in ROI evaluation and has earned the designation of certified performance technologist (CPT) and certified professional in learning and performance (CPLP). She has authored a number of publications on the subject of accountability and ROI, including *Show Me the Money: How to Determine ROI in People, Projects, and Programs* (Berrett-Koehler, 2007); *The Value of Learning* (Pfeiffer, 2007); *Return on Investment (ROI) Basics* (ASTD, 2005); *Proving the Value of HR: How and Why to Measure ROI* (Society for Human Resource Management, 2005); *Make Training Evaluation Work* (ASTD, 2004); *The Bottomline on ROI* (Center for Effective Performance, 2002), which won the 2003 ISPI Award of Excellence; *ROI at Work* (ASTD, 2005); the ASTD In Action casebooks *Measuring Return on Investment*, Volume 3 (2001), *Measuring ROI in the Public Sector* (2002), and *Retaining Your Best Employees* (2002); the ASTD Infoline series, including *Planning and Using Evaluation Data* (2003), *Mastering ROI* (1998), and *Managing Evaluation Shortcuts* (2001); and *The Human Resources Scorecard: Measuring Return on Investment* (Butterworth-Heinemann, 2001). Phillips's work has been published in a variety of journals. She can be reached at patti@roiinstitute.net.

Jack J. Phillips, Ph.D., a world-renowned expert on accountability, measurement, and evaluation, provides consulting services for Fortune 500 companies and major global organizations. The author or editor of more than fifty books, Phillips conducts workshops and makes conference presentations throughout the world.

His expertise in measurement and evaluation is based on more than twenty-seven years of corporate experience in the aerospace, textile, metals, construction materials, and banking industries. Phillips has served as training and development manager at two Fortune 500 firms, as senior human resources officer at two firms, as president of a regional bank, and as management professor at a major state university. This background led Phillips to develop the ROI Methodology, a revolutionary process that provides bottom-line figures and accountability for all types of learning, performance improvement, human resources, technology, and public policy programs.

Phillips regularly consults with clients in manufacturing, service, and government organizations in forty-four countries in North and South America, Europe, Africa, Australia, and Asia.

Books most recently authored by Phillips include *Show Me the Money: How to Determine ROI in People, Projects, and Programs* (Berrett-Koehler, 2007); *The Value of Learning* (Pfeiffer, 2007); *How to Build a Successful Consulting Practice* (McGraw-Hill, 2006); *Investing in Your Company's Human Capital: Strategies to Avoid Spending Too Much or Too Little* (Amacom, 2005); *Proving the Value of HR: How and Why to Measure ROI* (Society for Human Resource Management, 2005); *The Leadership Scorecard* (Butterworth-Heinemann, 2004); *Managing Employee Retention* (Butterworth-Heinemann, 2003); *Return on Investment in Training and Performance Improvement Programs*, 2nd edition (Butterworth-Heinemann, 2003); *The Project Management Scorecard* (Butterworth-Heinemann, 2002); *How to Measure Training Results* (McGraw-Hill, 2002); *The Human Resources Scorecard: Measuring the Return on Investment* (Butterworth-Heinemann, 2001); *The Consultant's Scorecard* (McGraw-Hill, 2000); and *Performance Analysis and Consulting* (ASTD, 2000). Phillips served as series editor for the In Action casebook series of the American Society for Training and Development (ASTD), an ambitious publishing project featuring thirty titles. He currently serves as series editor for Butterworth-Heinemann's Improving Human Performance series and for Pfeiffer's new Measurement and Evaluation series.

Phillips has received several awards for his books and his work. The Society for Human Resource Management presented him with an award for one of his books and honored a Phillips ROI study with its highest award for creativity. ASTD gave him its highest award, Distinguished Contribution to Workplace Learning and Development. *Meeting News* named Phillips one of the twenty-five most influential people in the meetings and events industry, based on his work on ROI within the industry.

Phillips holds undergraduate degrees in electrical engineering, physics, and mathematics; a master's degree in decision sciences from Georgia State University; and a Ph.D. degree in human resources management from the University of Alabama.

Jack Phillips has served on the boards of several private businesses—including two NASDAQ companies—and several associations, including ASTD, and nonprofit organizations. He is chairman of the ROI Institute, Inc., and can be reached at (205) 678-8101, or by e-mail at jack@roiinstitute.net.

Pfeiffer Publications Guide

This guide is designed to familiarize you with the various types of Pfeiffer publications. The formats section describes the various types of products that we publish; the methodologies section describes the many different ways that content might be provided within a product. We also provide a list of the topic areas in which we publish.

FORMATS

In addition to its extensive book-publishing program, Pfeiffer offers content in an array of formats, from fieldbooks for the practitioner to complete, ready-to-use training packages that support group learning.

FIELDBOOK Designed to provide information and guidance to practitioners in the midst of action. Most fieldbooks are companions to another, sometimes earlier, work, from which its ideas are derived; the fieldbook makes practical what was theoretical in the original text. Fieldbooks can certainly be read from cover to cover. More likely, though, you'll find yourself bouncing around following a particular theme, or dipping in as the mood, and the situation, dictate.

HANDBOOK A contributed volume of work on a single topic, comprising an eclectic mix of ideas, case studies, and best practices sourced by practitioners and experts in the field.

An editor or team of editors usually is appointed to seek out contributors and to evaluate content for relevance to the topic. Think of a handbook not as a ready-to-eat meal, but as a cookbook of ingredients that enables you to create the most fitting experience for the occasion.

RESOURCE Materials designed to support group learning. They come in many forms: a complete, ready-to-use exercise (such as a game); a comprehensive resource on one topic (such as conflict management) containing a variety of methods and approaches; or a collection of like-minded activities (such as icebreakers) on multiple subjects and situations.

TRAINING PACKAGE An entire, ready-to-use learning program that focuses on a particular topic or skill. All packages comprise a guide for the facilitator/trainer and a workbook for the participants. Some packages are supported with additional media—such as video—or learning aids, instruments, or other devices to help participants understand concepts or practice and develop skills.

- *Facilitator/trainer's guide* Contains an introduction to the program, advice on how to organize and facilitate the learning event, and step-by-step instructor notes. The guide also contains copies of presentation materials—handouts, presentations, and overhead designs, for example—used in the program.

- *Participant's workbook* Contains exercises and reading materials that support the learning goal and serves as a valuable reference and support guide for participants in the weeks and months that follow the learning event. Typically, each participant will require his or her own workbook.

ELECTRONIC CD-ROMs and web-based products transform static Pfeiffer content into dynamic, interactive experiences. Designed to take advantage of the searchability, automation, and ease-of-use that technology provides, our e-products bring convenience and immediate accessibility to your workspace.

METHODOLOGIES

CASE STUDY A presentation, in narrative form, of an actual event that has occurred inside an organization. Case studies are not prescriptive, nor are they used to prove a point; they are designed to develop critical analysis and decision-making skills. A case study has a specific time frame, specifies a sequence of events, is narrative in structure, and contains a plot structure—an issue (what should be/have been done?). Use case studies when the goal is to enable participants to apply previously learned theories to the circum-stances in the case, decide what is pertinent, identify the real issues, decide what should have been done, and develop a plan of action.

ENERGIZER A short activity that develops readiness for the next session or learning event. Energizers are most commonly used after a break or lunch to stimulate or refocus the group. Many involve some form of physical activity, so they are a useful way to counter post-lunch lethargy. Other uses include transitioning from one topic to another, where "mental" distancing is important.

EXPERIENTIAL LEARNING ACTIVITY (ELA) A facilitator-led intervention that moves participants through the learning cycle from experience to application (also known as a Structured Experience). ELAs are carefully thought-out designs in which there is a definite learning purpose and intended outcome. Each step—everything that participants do during the activity—facilitates the accomplishment of the stated goal. Each ELA includes complete instructions for facilitating the intervention and a clear statement of goals, suggested group size and timing, materials required, an explanation of the process, and, where appropriate, possible variations to the activity. (For more detail on Experiential Learning Activities, see the Introduction to the *Reference Guide to Handbooks and Annuals*, 1999 edition, Pfeiffer, San Francisco.)

GAME A group activity that has the purpose of fostering team spirit and togetherness in addition to the achievement of a pre-stated goal. Usually contrived—undertaking a desert expedition, for example—this type of learning method offers an engaging means for participants to demonstrate and practice business and interpersonal skills. Games are effective for team building and personal development mainly because the goal is subordinate to the process—the means through which participants reach decisions, collaborate, communicate, and generate trust and understanding. Games often engage teams in "friendly" competition.

ICEBREAKER A (usually) short activity designed to help participants overcome initial anxiety in a training session and/or to acquaint the participants with one another. An icebreaker can be a fun activity or can be tied to specific topics or training goals. While a useful tool in itself, the icebreaker comes into its own in situations where tension or resistance exists within a group.

INSTRUMENT A device used to assess, appraise, evaluate, describe, classify, and summarize various aspects of human behavior. The term used to describe an instrument depends primarily on its format and purpose. These terms include survey, questionnaire, inventory, diagnostic, survey, and poll. Some uses of instruments include providing instrumental feedback to group members, studying here-and-now processes or functioning within a group, manipulating group composition, and evaluating outcomes of training and other interventions.

Instruments are popular in the training and HR field because, in general, more growth can occur if an individual is provided with a method for focusing specifically on his or her own behavior. Instruments also are used to obtain information that will serve as a basis for change and to assist in workforce planning efforts.

Paper-and-pencil tests still dominate the instrument landscape with a typical package comprising a facilitator's guide, which offers advice on administering the instrument and interpreting the collected data, and an initial set of instruments. Additional instruments are available separately. Pfeiffer, though, is investing heavily in e-instruments. Electronic instrumentation provides effortless distribution and, for larger groups particularly, offers advantages over paper-and-pencil tests in the time it takes to analyze data and provide feedback.

LECTURETTE A short talk that provides an explanation of a principle, model, or process that is pertinent to the participants' current learning needs. A lecturette is intended to establish a common language bond between the trainer and the participants by providing a mutual frame of reference. Use a lecturette as an introduction to a group activity or event, as an interjection during an event, or as a handout.

MODEL A graphic depiction of a system or process and the relationship among its elements. Models provide a frame of reference and something more tangible, and more easily remembered, than a verbal explanation. They also give participants something to "go on," enabling them to track their own progress as they experience the dynamics, processes, and relationships being depicted in the model.

ROLE PLAY A technique in which people assume a role in a situation/ scenario: a customer service rep in an angry-customer exchange, for example. The way in which the role is approached is then discussed and feedback is offered. The role play is often repeated using a different approach and/or incorporating changes made based on feedback received. In other words, role playing is a spontaneous interaction involving realistic behavior under artificial (and safe) conditions.

SIMULATION A methodology for understanding the interrelationships among components of a system or process. Simulations differ from games in that they test or use a model that depicts or mirrors some aspect of reality in form, if not necessarily in content. Learning occurs by studying the effects of change on one or more factors of the model. Simulations are commonly used to test hypotheses about what happens in a system—often referred to as "what if?" analysis—or to examine best-case/worst-case scenarios.

THEORY A presentation of an idea from a conjectural perspective. Theories are useful because they encourage us to examine behavior and phenomena through a different lens.

TOPICS

The twin goals of providing effective and practical solutions for workforce training and organization development and meeting the educational needs of training and human resource professionals shape Pfeiffer's publishing program. Core topics include the following:

    Leadership & Management

    Communication & Presentation

    Coaching & Mentoring

    Training & Development

    E-Learning

    Teams & Collaboration

    OD & Strategic Planning

    Human Resources

    Consulting

What will you find on pfeiffer.com?

- The best in workplace performance solutions for training and HR professionals

- Downloadable training tools, exercises, and content

- Web-exclusive offers

- Training tips, articles, and news

- Seamless on-line ordering

- Author guidelines, information on becoming a Pfeiffer Affiliate, and much more

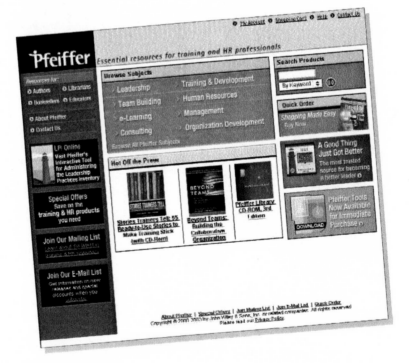

Discover more at www.pfeiffer.com

Measurement and Evaluation Series

Series Editors
Patricia Pulliam Phillips, Ph.D., and Jack J. Phillips, Ph.D.

A six-book set that provides a step-by-step system for planning, measuring, calculating, and communicating evaluation and Return-on-Investment for training and development, featuring:

- Detailed templates
- Complete plans
- Ready-to-use tools
- Real-world case examples

The M&E Series features:

1. *ROI Fundamentals: Why and When to Measure ROI*
   (978-0-7879-8716-9)

2. *Data Collection: Planning For and Collecting All Types of Data*
   (978-0-7879-8718-3)

3. *Isolation of Results: Defining the Impact of the Program*
   (978-0-7879-8719-0)

4. *Data Conversion: Calculating the Monetary Benefits*
   (978-0-7879-8720-6)

5. *Costs and ROI: Evaluating at the Ultimate Level*
   (978-0-7879-8721-3)

6. *Communication and Implementation: Sustaining the Practice*
   (978-0-7879-8722-0)

Plus, the *ROI in Action Casebook* (978-0-7879-8717-6) covers all the major workplace learning and performance applications, including Leadership Development, Sales Training, Performance Improvement, Technical Skills Training, Information Technology Training, Orientation and OJT, and Supervisor Training.

The **ROI Methodology** is a comprehensive measurement and evaluation process that collects six types of measures: Reaction, Satisfaction, and Planned Action; Learning; Application and Implementation; Business Impact; Return on Investment; and Intangible Measures. The process provides a step-by-step system for evaluation and planning, data collection, data analysis, and reporting. It is appropriate for the measurement and evaluation of *all* kinds of performance improvement programs and activities, including training and development, learning, human resources, coaching, meetings and events, consulting, and project management.

Special Offer from the ROI Institute

Send for your own ROI Process Model, an indispensable tool for implementing and presenting ROI in your organization. The ROI Institute is offering an exclusive gift to readers of The Measurement and Evaluation Series. This 11"×25" multicolor foldout shows the ROI Methodology flow model and the key issues surrounding the implementation of the ROI Methodology. This easy-to-understand overview of the ROI Methodology has proven invaluable to countless professionals when implementing the ROI Methodology. Please return this page or e-mail your information to the address below to receive your free foldout (a $6.00 value). Please check your area(s) of interest in ROI.

Please send me the ROI Process Model described in the book. I am interested in learning more about the following ROI materials and services:

☐ Workshops and briefing on ROI   ☐ ROI consulting services
☐ Books and support materials on ROI   ☐ ROI Network information
☐ Certification in the ROI Methodology   ☐ ROI benchmarking
☐ ROI software   ☐ ROI research

Name _____

Title _____

Organization _____

Address _____

Phone _____

E-mail Address _____

Functional area of interest:

☐ Learning and Development/Performance Improvement
☐ Human Resources/Human Capital
☐ Public Relations/Community Affairs/Government Relations
☐ Consulting
☐ Sales/Marketing
☐ Technology/IT Systems
☐ Project Management Solutions
☐ Quality/Six Sigma
☐ Operations/Methods/Engineering
☐ Research and Development/Innovations
☐ Finance/Compliance
☐ Logistics/Distribution/Supply Chain
☐ Public Policy Initiatives
☐ Social Programs
☐ Other (Please Specify) _____

Organizational Level

☐ executive   ☐ management   ☐ consultant   ☐ specialist
☐ student   ☐ evaluator   ☐ researcher

Return this form or contact   The ROI Institute
                                     P.O. Box 380637
                                     Birmingham, AL 35238-0637

Or e-mail information to info@roiinstitute.net
Please allow four to six weeks for delivery.